the backyard astronomer

the backyard astronomer

a guide to stargazing

DENNIS L. MAMMANA

MetroBooks

To Candace, into whose eyes I'd much rather be gazing. . .

MetroBooks

An Imprint of Friedman/Fairfax Publishers

Library of Congress Cataloging-in-Publication Data available upon request.

ISBN 1-56799-343-5

Editor: Karla Olson
Art Director: Jeff Batzli
Designer: Terry Peterson
Photography Editor: Emilya Naymark

Color separations by HBM Print Ltd.
Printed in China by Leefung-Asco Printers Ltd.

For bulk purchases and special sales, please contact:
Friedman/Fairfax Publishers
Attention: Sales Department
15 West 26th Street
New York, NY 10010
212/685-6610 FAX 212/685-1307

Contents

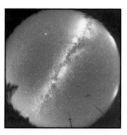

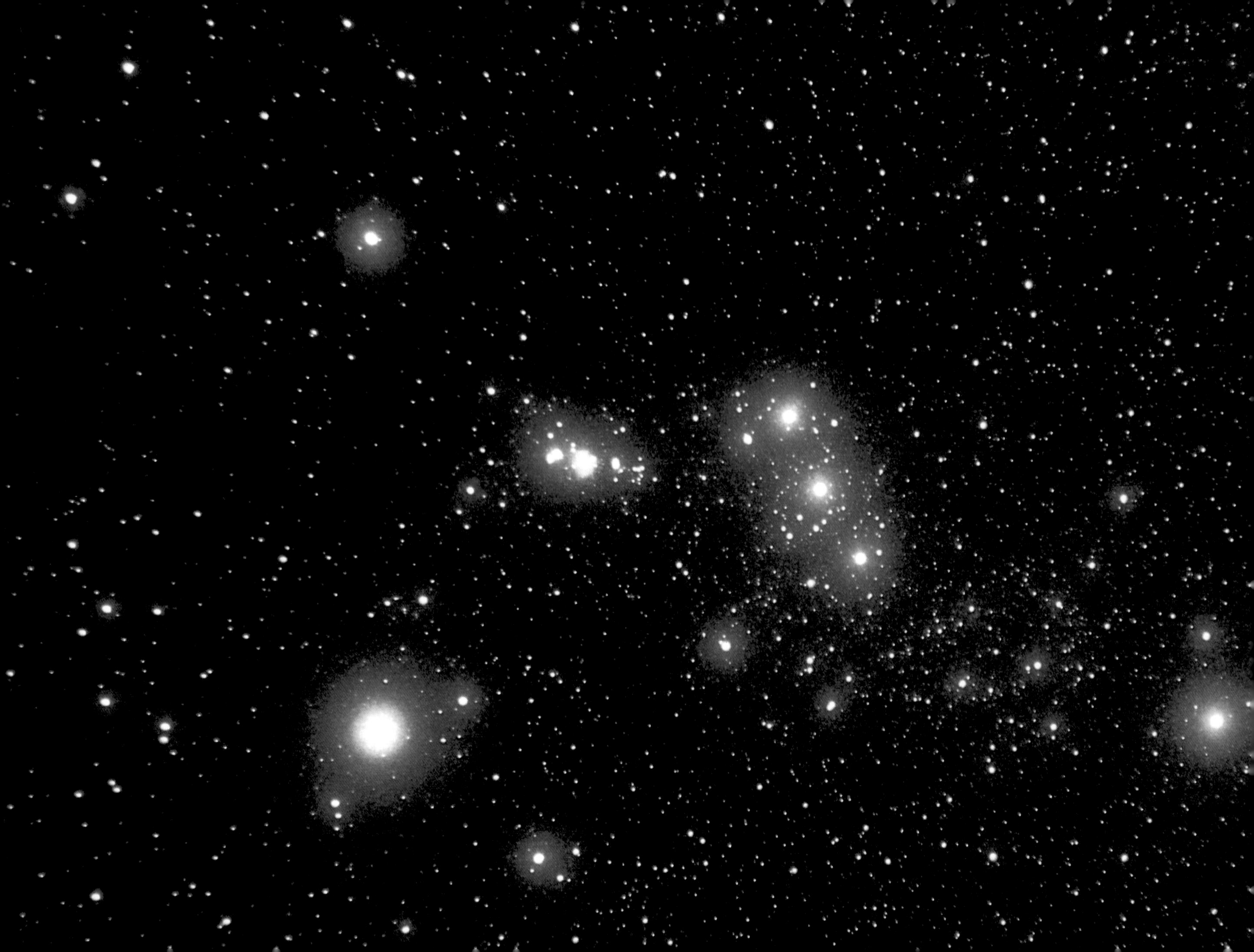

Chapter *1*

What Are the Stars?

Chances are, until now you've looked up into the night sky and seen two things—the moon and many, many stars. If you live in the Northern Hemisphere, you've probably picked out the Big Dipper and the Little Dipper; from the Southern Hemisphere, you might have found the stars of Crux or Alpha and Beta Centauri. Otherwise, all the stars twinkling in the night probably look the same to you.

However, if you look more closely, you will realize that there are all kinds of distinctions to be made between the different points of light that are shining in the sky. Some are brighter than others, and some have a definite color. Some are twinkling, while others burn with a steady light. Pretty soon you will see that every star in the heavens has a unique personality, and you will be able to classify the stars into categories and types, and find them again and again as you watch the stars move through the sky.

Naming the Stars

One way to begin to differentiate the pinpoints in the sky is to learn their names. Every star is given an official designation, which consists of a number that indicates either the star's position in the sky or its entry in a particular catalog. Some stars have several designations, indicating different qualities, characteristics, and

*Left: Orion, the Hunter—with its three distinctive "belt" stars—is one of the brightest and most recognized constellations in the heavens. **Above:** One of the most spectacular star clusters—the Pleiades, or the Seven Sisters—rides on the back of Taurus, the Bull.*

position in the sky. For instance, the star HD172167 might also be known as SA067174 or BD+38°83238, depending on how the observer is categorizing it.

Stars are also designated by a Greek letter followed by a Latin constellation name. For instance, HD172167 is also known as Alpha Lyrae. The Greek letter indicates the brightness of the star, alpha being the brightest, followed by beta, gamma, delta, epsilon, and so on, in order of diminishing brightness.

Vega shines with a distinctive white color and lies 150 trillion miles (240 trillion km) away.

What's in a Name?

Just as the numbers and letters assigned to different stars may indicate their position in the sky, the meanings of their proper names sometimes contain clues to their place in the heavens. Most star names are taken from classical Arabic and are very revealing.

Name	Meaning	Position
Deneb	tail	at the back of the constellation Cygnus, the Swan
Betelgeuse	armpit of the giant	near the shoulder of the constellation Orion, the Hunter

---

The constellation name specifies the area of the sky in which the star can be found—in this case Lyra, the constellation known as the Harp. So, Alpha Lyrae is the brightest star in Lyra, the Harp.

The best and most accessible way to get to know the stars is to learn their proper names. HD172167, for example, is also called Vega, which is much easier to remember than a long list of numbers or complicated Greek and Latin. Just as you remember people's names after you have met them and have come to know them a bit, you will come to learn the differences between the stars and start to recognize them by their proper names.

Classifying by Brightness

Another way to distinguish stars from one another is by their relative brightness. If you look closely at the night sky, you will see that some stars shine more brightly than others, and some twinkle more than others. Don't make the common mistake of believing that you can judge how close to Earth a star is by considering its brightness alone. True, a star's brightness is determined by how close it is, but also by how much light it actually emits. For instance, the planets often shine brighter than the stars in the sky, a result of their relative proximity to Earth. However, they have no source of light themselves, but reflect the sun's light. On the other hand, Rigel, which is the

brightest star in Orion, shines 50,000 times more brightly than the sun and has a diameter 30 times as great; however, because Rigel is 1,400 light-years away from Earth, it does not seem—to the untrained eye—to be brighter than some planets.

So how do stargazers measure the "apparent" brightness of a star? They use a numerical scale called "magnitude," in a system first developed by an ancient Greek astronomer named Hipparchus. Hipparchus organized the stars into six categories, 1st being the brightest and 6th the faintest. Each magnitude is 2.514 times fainter than the next. In other words, a 2nd-magnitude star is 2.514 times fainter than a 1st-magnitude, and a 5th-magnitude star is 39.94 times (2.514 × 2.514 × 2.514 × 2.514) fainter than a 1st-magnitude star. Hipparchus classified the faintest stars as 6th magnitude, 100 times fainter than the brightest stars.

Keep in mind that Hipparchus was working at a time when he could observe the sky with nothing more powerful than the naked eye, and he was convinced that there were no stars fainter than 6th magnitude. Obviously, he would be amazed at what we know today. Even with the first telescopes, developed in the seventeenth century, astronomers discovered that there are actually more stars that are fainter than 6th magnitude than there are brighter ones. They called any star just beyond visibility 7th magnitude, and began to classify them from there on. Today the most powerful telescopes can see stars as faint as 25th magnitude—39 million times (2.514 times itself 19 times) fainter than those visible to the naked eye.

When astronomers began to analyze Hipparchus' categories of brightness more closely, they found that he had lumped together in the 1st magnitude the brightest stars with the planets and the sun. Of course, the degrees of brightness of these celestial objects are very different, so they expanded the magnitude categories in the opposite direction as well. Stars 2.514 times brighter than Hipparchus' 1st-magnitude stars became 0 magnitude. Those 2.514 times brighter still became -1 magnitude, and so on. With this system, the moon is categorized at -12.7 magnitude, while the sun is a remarkable -26.7 magnitude.

In the high-tech world of modern astronomy, stellar brightness is measured with electronic detectors called "photometers." Even so, with practice, brightness can be estimated by the naked eye. The trick is to compare an unknown star's brightness with that of a known star. For instance, in the Northern Hemisphere, it is easy to measure stellar magnitude relative to the stars in the bowl of the Little Dipper. Conveniently, its bowl contains

The center of our Milky Way Galaxy, visible in the direction of the constellation Sagittarius, may hide a massive black hole from view.

four stars, each of a different magnitude, from 2nd to 5th. This provides a basis of comparison for other stars in the sky. Although Southern Hemisphere observers don't have a star grouping that is directly comparable to the Little Dipper, they can look toward any familiar grouping of stars and find examples of each.

Furthermore, because the Little Dipper is often obscured by bright city lights or moonlight, it can act as a gauge to the viewing quality of the sky on a given night or from a particular location. If you can see only the brightest star in the Little Dipper, this is an indication that you won't be able to discern any stars fainter than 2nd magnitude—not a good night or location from which to search for faint constellations such as Cancer or Delphinus. If, on the other hand, you can see three or four of the bowl stars, your visibility is down to 4th or 5th magnitude, and you should be able to see stars down to that brightness.

The farthest object visible to the naked eye—the great galaxy in Andromeda— appears much as our Milky Way would from its tremendous distance.

What Is a Light-Year?

The moon is 240,000 miles (384,000km) away from Earth. The sun is 93 million miles (149 million km) away. As incomprehensible as these distances are, they are nothing compared to the distances of the stars. Proxima Centauri, the nearest star—visible to those in the Southern Hemisphere—is 26 trillion miles (41.5 trillion km) from Earth. Beyond this star are the millions of pinpoints that make up the Milky Way, which stretches for 600,000 trillion miles (960,000 trillion km) from end to end. Beyond the Milky Way are even more galaxies, only a minute percentage of which are visible to the strongest telescopes; some of these are estimated to be as distant as 100 billion trillion miles (160 billion trillion km) into space.

Astronomers use the speed of light to help gauge cosmic mileage. Light is the fastest-traveling substance known, moving at a speed of 186,000 miles (297,600km) per second, or more than 11 million

Object	Distance in Light-Years	Constellation
Sirius	9	Canis Major (the Big Dog)
Altair	16	Aquila (the Eagle)
Arcturus	34	Bootes (the Herdsman)
Regulus	69	Leo (the Lion)
Dubhe	100	Ursa Major (the Great Bear)
Spica	220	Virgo (the Maiden)
Pleiades Cluster	410	Taurus (the Bull)
Polaris	820	Ursa Minor (the Little Bear)
Alphirk	1,000	Cepheus (the King)
Deneb	1,500	Cygnus (the Swan)
Al Anz	2,800	Auriga (the Charioteer)
Andromeda Galaxy	2,000,000	Andromeda (the Daughter of Cepheus and Cassiopeia)

miles (17.5 million km) a minute, through the vacuum of space. Even at that speed, light takes a significant amount of time to travel from where it first glistened to where we on Earth can see it. It takes 1.3 seconds for us to see light from the moon, and 8.3 minutes for us to see sunlight or feel its warmth. Light from Proxima Centauri travels for 4.3 years before it reaches Earth, so we say it lies 4.3 light-years away. The Milky Way stretches some

100,000 light-years across the sky, and the farthest known objects in the sky may lie some 15 to 18 billion light-years away from Earth. Although these numbers quickly become incomprehensible, thinking in light-years makes it easier to understand objects' relative distance from Earth.

It is mind-boggling to contemplate these places as they were when they released the light we perceive on Earth today. Consider

the summertime star Deneb, which lies 1,500 light-years away; we are seeing it today as it was near the end of the fourth century, during the fall of the Roman Empire. The farthest object visible to the naked eye is the fuzzy patch of light near the northeastern corner of the Square of Pegasus—the Great Galaxy of the Andromeda—some 2 million light-years away. That means that we see it as it was long before humans inhabited Earth.

Color

Stars are categorized not only by their brightness, but also by their color. Unlike brightness, a factor that depends on a star's intrinsic luminosity and its distance from Earth, the color of a star is determined by its temperature. A star glows much the same as molten steel or glass does when it is heated. As its temperature rises, it appears red-hot at first, then orange, yellow, white, and finally blue.

Many stars, like the sun, are white stars; that is, their gases shine at a temperature around 10,000°F (5,500°C). Cooler stars—those with temperatures of 5,000 to 6,000°F (2,750 to 3,300°C)—appear to our eyes as reddish or orange. The hottest stars we can see with the naked eye burn at 20,000 to 30,000°F (11,100 to 16,500°C) and appear to be bluish white.

Color perception is a very subjective thing, as it is dependent on viewing conditions and the accuracy of the viewer's own color receptors. Still, color perception can be helpful to people who are learning their way around the heavens.

*Left: Taurus, the Bull, shows stars of distinctly different colors. **Below:** The Big Dipper forms the most famous shape in the Northern Hemisphere sky.*

Twinkle, Twinkle, Little Star

As the old nursery rhyme points out, many of the stars seem to twinkle like diamonds in the sky. This is not because of any fluctuation in the light that they emit; the "twinkling" is caused by the indirect route the light takes through our planet's atmosphere. As it journeys, the light is bounced around by moving air surrounding Earth, making the eye perceive that the light is fading and brightening, or twinkling. Stars low in the sky twinkle even more than their overhead companions because their light has traveled through so much more of the atmosphere.

Kinds of Stars

The more you gaze up into the sky, the more different kinds of celestial phenomena you will discover. Double stars, variable stars, meteors, comets, and zodiacal lights are just a few of the sights you will find.

Double Stars

You are looking at a star in the sky and suddenly realize that it has a twin or a bright "shadow." Most of these "double stars" are actually optical illusions caused by two stars appearing along nearly the same line of vision. Even so, they are intriguing.

One of the most famous double stars is located in the Northern Hemisphere grouping of the Big Dipper. Right at the curve of the handle are Alcor and Mizar, often called the Horse and Rider. The ancient Arabs used this pair of stars as an eyesight test for someone trying to enlist in the army; if the applicant could see the two stars, then his eyesight was good enough for him to join the troops.

Other double stars are not quite so easy to spot with the naked eye. Epsilon

Lyrae, for example, the faint star just to the east of the brilliant summer star Vega, in Lyra, the Harp, is also double. However, only observers with terrific eyesight on nights with excellent sky transparency can make out this pair without a telescope.

Variable Stars

Not all stars appear at the same brightness all the time. Even the well-known Polaris, the North Star, has variable brightness. Some change just slightly, while others change more dramatically. Delta Cephei changes in brightness from 3.5 magnitude to 4.4 magnitude in a little more than 5 days. It does so because it is actually swelling and contracting.

The apparent brightness of some variable stars changes more slowly, often because of instabilities within their atmospheres. Omicron Ceti, also known as Mira the Wonderful, goes from easy visibility (magnitude 2.0) to invisibility (magnitude 10.1) in 332 days.

A given star may change in brightness because another star that is in orbit around it passes in front of it and temporarily blocks it from view. These stars are called "eclipsing binary stars." One of the most famous eclipsing binaries is known as Algol, the Demon Star, or Beta Persei; this star changes in brightness from magnitude 2.1 to 3.3 in just 3 days.

Omicron Ceti is the prototype of the class of variable stars known as long-period variables.

With the exception of lunar samples returned by Apollo astronauts, meteorites represent the only samples of other worlds that scientists can analyze in the lab.

Naming Variable Stars

When a variable star is named, it is assigned a letter, from R through Z, followed by the name of the constellation to which the star belongs. The first variable star found in Sagittarius is named R Sagittarii. The next is named S Sagittarii, the one after that T Sagittarii, and so on. When Z is reached, the letters start again with R and a second letter, also beginning with R, e.g., RR, RS, RT. When ZZ is reached, the letters move to the beginning of the alphabet: AA, AB, AC, and so on. (The single letters A through Q are not used, as they had already been employed to name newly discovered stars in the Southern Hemisphere sky.) In this way, 334 variable stars can be designated in any one constellation. But often more are needed, so instead of continuing with the triple-letter combination, astronomers continue with V335, V336, V337, making an infinite number of variable stars catalogable. And how many are needed? More than 1,134 have been cataloged in Sagittarius alone.

Meteors

Meteors are specks of dust—sometimes smaller than a grain of sand—that fall from space into our atmosphere. As these specks, moving at tens of miles per second, encounter the air, friction heats them up to thousands of degrees and they vaporize in a flash.

While these specks are tumbling through space, they are known as "meteoroids." When they plunge into the outer atmosphere and burn up, they are referred to as "meteors." If they are large enough to survive their fiery descent and plunge to Earth, they are known as "meteorites." Meteorites are few and far between; only about 2,000 have been found around the world.

Even the very smallest meteor is quite spectacular as it falls through the air. Some move very quickly, while others barely drift. Like stars, their colors range over the spectrum: white, orange, red, blue, and green. Some leave behind smoke trails or even cast a shadow; these are called "fireballs." Others, known as "bolides," whistle, sizzle, or even create a sonic boom as they fall.

As Earth moves through its orbit around the sun, it occasionally encounters swarms of meteoric particles, most of which have been left along the orbits of ancient comets. As Earth plows forward into these particles, an observer on the ground might see as many as two meteors falling from the sky every minute. These meteors all seem to come from one general direction in the sky, called the "radiant" of the shower. The radiant is named for the constellation that appears behind it: Leonids, Orionids, and Geminids, among others.

Earth meets these swarms of meteors several times a year (see chart on page 15). One of the most reliable is the Perseids shower (named for the constellation Perseus), which occurs every year in mid-August. On a clear, dark night, Perseid watchers can see at least four dozen meteors falling from the sky every hour. To get the best view of any shower, watch the skies after midnight, as this is the time when Earth is facing in the direction of its motion through space. Pull up a lounge chair, cover up with a blanket or crawl into a sleeping bag, sit back, and enjoy.

*Above, left: The Leonids shower can be one of the most exciting of the year. **Above, right:** Meteor Crater, created so recently that erosion and geological processes have not yet erased it from view, is open to the public.*

Principal Meteor Showers

Date of Maximum*	Shower Name	Best Time to Watch	Hourly Rate**	Associated Comet
January 4	Quadrantids	before dawn	40–150	—
April 21	Lyrids	before dawn	10–15	1861 I
May 4	Eta Aquarids	before dawn	10–40	Halley
July 30	Delta Aquarids	before dawn	10–35	—
August 11–13	Perseids	before dawn	50–100	1862 III
October 9	Draconids	evening	10	Giacobini-Zinner
October 20	Orionids	before dawn	10–70	Halley
November 9	Taurids	midnight	5–15	Encke
November 16	Leonids	before dawn	5–20	1866 I
November 25–27	Andromedids	evening	10	Biela
December 13	Geminids	before dawn	50–80	—
December 22	Ursids	before dawn	10–15	—

*Date of actual maximum occurrence may vary by 1 or 2 days in either direction.

**Hourly rate refers to the number of meteors you can expect to see per hour. The hourly rate varies from year to year.

Meteor Lore

Although meteors very rarely fall to Earth, when they do they make a big bang, physically or culturally. Fifty thousand years ago, a chunk of iron as big as a house fell to Earth in what is now northern Arizona. It ripped a hole 4,000 feet (1.2km) wide and 600 feet (183m) deep, now known as Meteor Crater.

Long ago, meteorites were considered sacred by some Native American tribes. They wrapped them in cloth and buried them with other valuable possessions. In 1492, a meteorite fell in a small town in France, where it was displayed in a church and worshiped as a sign from God. Today, astronomers study meteorites for what they can reveal about other places in our solar system. They believe that most are pieces of asteroids, the moon, or Mars. Some might even be pieces of passing comets.

Long ago, comets were believed to be harbingers of doom. Today, scientists welcome comets so that we can glean insights into the origin of our solar system.

Comets

Comets are chunks of ice and rock that orbit the sun in the depths of our solar system—far beyond the orbit of Pluto—and cannot be seen with even the strongest telescope. Occasionally, however, the gravity of the sun or one of the giant planets tugs a comet inward, forcing it to swing past Earth. As it does, the sun's light and heat vaporize its ices, and the solar wind blows the cometary material outward into what we see as a long and beautiful tail.

Half a dozen or so new comets are discovered each year. Most are found by backyard comet hunters, and they are named for their discoverers. However, only the very nearest and brightest of these can be seen by the naked eye. Some comets, such as Comet Ikeya-Seki (1965) are dazzling, their brilliant tails stretching completely across the sky. Others, such as Comet Kohoutek (1973), are a disappointment, as they are barely visible.

A bright comet drifting majestically among the stars is one of the most magnificent sights in nature. Perhaps the most famous of all is Halley's Comet, which orbits the sun every 76 years. During its last visit, in 1986, Halley's Comet was not very bright, for it never came that close to Earth. The next time it will come to visit is 2062.

Zodiacal Light

Scattered between the planets and stars is a tremendous amount of debris left over from the birth of our planetary family 5 billion years ago. This debris, which scatters the sunlight of our solar system, creates two fascinating astronomical phenomena.

The first is zodiacal light, which can best be seen in the Northern Hemisphere in March, and in the Southern Hemisphere in September, as a hazy triangular band or cone stretching upward from the western horizon after dark. In the autumn months of both hemispheres (September in the Northern and March in the Southern), this cone reaches upward from the horizon in the eastern sky before dawn.

The second phenomenon is known as *gegenschein*, or "counterglow." You can see the counterglow at about midnight during the months from September to November in the constellation Pisces, the Fish. During January and February it occurs, also at about midnight, within Cancer, the Crab. Look for a faint, somewhat elliptical glow about 10 degrees in width.

The debris that causes this astronomical glow is minute dust particles, less than 1 millionth of an inch in diameter. Therefore, the particles are extremely faint and can be seen under only the very best conditions. The best way to view them is on a moonless night in a location without haze or even light pollution.

Asteroids

An asteroid, also known as a minor planet, is any small rocky body that orbits the sun. The largest asteroid in our solar system is Ceres, which is 480 miles (768km) in diameter. Most asteroids are found in the asteroid belt that exists between Mars and Jupiter.

Like planets, asteroids can be seen from Earth because they reflect the light of the sun. However, they are much

The triangular glow appearing near Comet Ikeya-Seki is called the zodiacal light. It is caused by the reflection of sunlight from myriad dust particles along the plane of our solar system.

fainter than the planets because their reflective surface is so much smaller. The first asteroid discovered was Ceres, in 1801, followed by Pallas (1802), Juno (1804), and Vesta (1807). We now know that there are thousands of asteroids in the asteroid belt. Most are irregular in shape, and scientists theorize that they are actually parts of a planet that was unable to form because of disruptive forces from Jupiter's gravitational pull.

There are a number of asteroids whose orbits take them very close to Earth—within 10 million miles (16 million km). In June 1968, Icarus passed within 3 million miles (4.8 million km), and in 1937, Hermes passed within half a million miles (800,000km). Recently, asteroid 1991 BA, discovered in January 1991, came within 102,000 miles (163,200km) and was closely watched by astronomers around the world. It was determined that asteroid 1991 BA was no more than 40 miles (64km) in diameter; even so, if it had hit Earth, the impact could have been disastrous.

You Named an Asteroid After *Him*!?

Lucky are the people who discover asteroids, for they get to choose any name for their discovery that they like. Each newly sighted asteroid is assigned a number that indicates its place in the long list of asteroids. Then the discoverer chooses any name he or she would like to attach to that number. When asteroids were first named, most astronomers selected names from mythology, usually those of female figures. Later, they chose names of characters from Shakespeare's plays or Wagner's operas. Today, asteroids, like roses, are named after husbands, wives, children, pets, friends, famous people, and even popular music groups. (There is an asteroid named after the Beatles.) It's never too early to start thinking of whom you might honor by naming an asteroid after him or her!

Left: Ida, a 32-mile (51.2km)-long asteroid, was photographed by the Galileo spacecraft on its way toward Jupiter.

Man-Made Satellites

Only hundreds of miles out in space, hundreds of man-made satellites are orbiting Earth. Because they are made of metal that reflects sunlight, they are easy to see; they look just like stars, except that they move. Because they are in orbit and are not just masses that burn up upon impact with the atmosphere, they move much more slowly than meteors, and they don't burn out. If you think you see a satellite, look carefully; if the object has red and green flashing lights, it is an airplane.

Try to determine the direction in which a satellite is moving. If it is drifting from east to west or west to east, it was probably put up by the Americans. Russian satellites often move from south to north and north to south. Some brighten and fade as they orbit, which means that they are spinning or tumbling along their course.

It takes a satellite about ninety minutes to orbit Earth, and along its course it performs various duties, from tracking the weather to sending telephone and radio waves to collecting information.

One of the brightest of all satellites is the Russian MIR Space Station.

Left and above: Though many photographs have been taken of UFOs, few are clear and sharp enough to identify their true nature.

Although it appears tiny, it is large enough to be home to several cosmonauts or astronauts.

UFOs

Looking into the heavens and seeing all the stars that exist, it seems virtually impossible to deny that there must be life in at least a few of those distant places. Man has always been fascinated with the possibility that creatures from other solar systems might come to visit our planet, or that we might visit theirs. Perhaps interstellar or intergalactic travel will become a reality someday.

Today, however, there is no evidence on Earth of any kind of alien contact or life. Yet how does one explain the hundreds of sightings of Unidentified Flying Objects (UFOs) every year? Although this reality is not as romantic or dramatic as the explanations imagination can create, most UFOs are simply observations made by people who are not familiar with the skies and don't understand what they are seeing. UFOs usually turn out to be aircraft, satellites, meteors, searchlights, clouds, or bright stars or planets that are exhibiting a particularly spectacular display. Experienced astronomers recognize these things for what they are, while those less familiar with the sky often let their imaginations run wild.

That doesn't mean that you won't someday see something particularly exciting or dramatic that you cannot explain. When you do, don't panic—keep your head and record all you can about the object or phenomenon: date and time, location from which you see it, location of the object or phenomenon in the sky, conditions of the sky, speed of the object, direction of its motion, color, and brightness. Also, try to take a photo or video. This information will help you and the authorities turn that UFO into an IFO—Identified Flying Object.

❋

These are just a few of the many things you will witness as you explore the heavens. It is possible that you will become familiar with all of them, with their individual movements and behaviors. You will welcome them like old friends when they appear for a visit to your viewing skies, and bid them a fond farewell as they push on with their journeys.

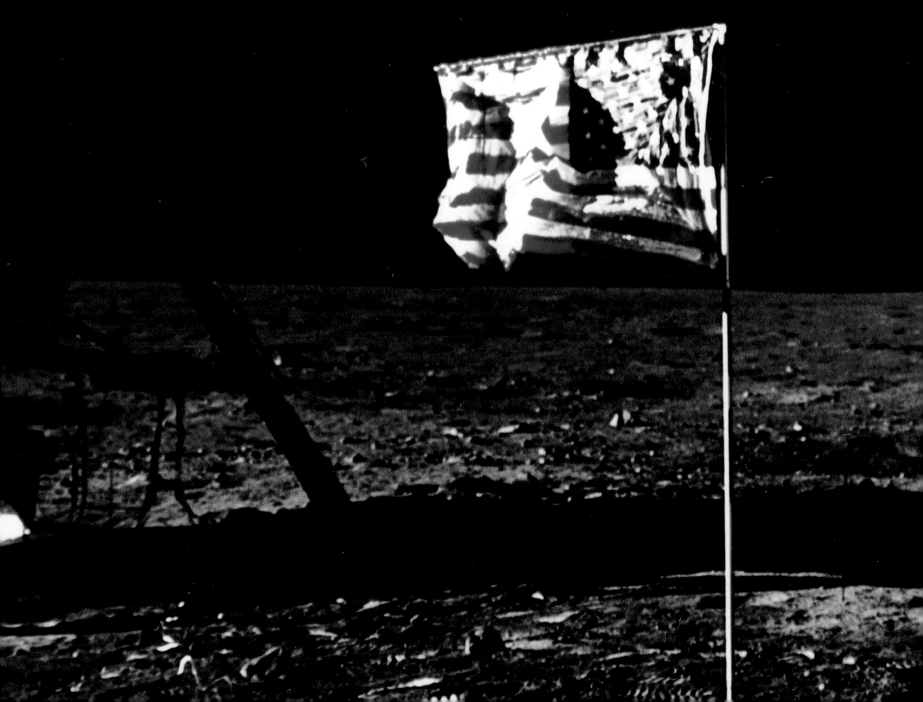

Chapter *2*

Our Constant Companion—the Moon

A bright-eyed child waits impatiently for the sun to set. She knows that, even before bedtime, she may catch a glimpse of the Man in the Moon. She will welcome him with joy and excitement, calling his name in the dark. She has come to expect to see his shining face every night, and she considers him an old friend. He is the night-light shining in the heavens that tells her all is right with her world.

Humans have always been fascinated by the moon's cycles and characteristics. The moon is a fundamental part of our experience of life on Earth, and one that helps us through each day. The moon brightens the darkness of night and indicates the passage of time and the consistent cycles that we all experience. It is also the object with which most beginning astronomers are already familiar.

There is so much to learn and observe by watching the moon from night to night. What is its position in the sky relative to the other things you see, and where will it be tomorrow night? What is its shape, and what does that indicate about the lunar cycle? What makes the faces on the moon? What are eclipses and when do they occur? These are but a few of the many questions you can answer by watching the moon every night.

Lunar Position

Every 29.5 days, the moon moves—west to east—once through its elliptical orbit around Earth. Earth is not in the center

Left: The second man to step on the moon, Edwin "Buzz" Aldrin, looks at the U.S. flag he planted on the lunar surface on July 20, 1969. Above: Our nearest neighbor, the moon, has been worshiped and studied since humans first looked skyward millennia ago.

A fine time to observe the dark "maria" on the lunar surface is when the full moon is rising in the east.

of this orbit, but more to one end. The moon has a "perigee"—the point at which it is closest to Earth in its orbit, about 221,000 miles (353,600km)—and an "apogee"—the point at which it is farthest away from Earth, about 253,000 miles (404,800km). All the way through its cycle, from the perigee to the apogee and back to the perigee, the moon travels more than 1 million miles (1.6 million km)—in less than 30 days.

This means that the moon must move approximately 12 degrees eastward every day. Knowing this, it is easy to predict its position from night to night. Begin by noting its exact position relative to a constant object, from the same place and at precisely the same time several nights in a row. You will observe it moving farther to the east. One night, with your fist at arm's length, measure a distance one fist-width (this will be about 10 degrees, as explained on page 23) to the east; this will be the approximate position of the moon the following night. Note the position on a star map, then check your prediction the next night. You will soon learn how to refine your predictions.

Foreground objects make it possible to easily measure of the moon's motion during the night.

You can make the same kind of prediction about the moon's position in the sky during the course of a night. Moving 12 degrees a day means that the moon must move half a degree an hour, or about one full-moon diameter. To see this, once again mark the moon's position relative to some nearby stars on your star map. About an hour later, check its place again, and you should see that it has moved one full diameter.

What Is a Degree?

Technically speaking, a degree is $\frac{1}{360}$ of a circle, but what does that mean to an observer of the night sky? As the sky is a circular shape from horizon to horizon, a measurement that is based on a circle is a good one by which to measure objects in the sky and their distance from one another. Like a circle, the sky can be divided into 360 equal pieces, and each one is 1 degree wide.

Using your finger or fist to measure sizes and speeds of celestial objects helps to make the universe seem less overwhelming.

But how do you measure a degree when you are out looking at the sky? Simply hold your little finger at arm's length—its width is equal to approximately 1 degree. A thumb held at arm's length is approximately 2 degrees wide, three fingers are approximately 5 degrees wide, and a fist is approximately 10 degrees wide. The distance between the tip of your thumb and the tip of your pinky is approximately 15 degrees, or the distance between the two outside stars in the Big Dipper.

Of course, these figures are rough because everyone's fingers and hands are different sizes. If you want to be more accurate, measure the width of your fist or little finger. Then measure its distance from your eye when at arm's length. Divide the width by the distance, and multiply the total by 57.3. This will give you a more accurate measure of just how many degrees or how much of a degree your fist or your finger represents. Whenever you measure off a distance, multiply the number of fist or finger widths by this number.

Lunar Phases

We have all seen the moon's different shapes, from the sliver of a new moon to the round glory of a full moon. These "phases," as they are called, occur because the moon is illuminated from different angles by the sun. As you watch the moon from night to night, you will become familiar with what these phases indicate about the position of the moon in its continuing cycle. As you watch the moon through its phases, keep in mind that someone on the moon would see Earth go through the same (but opposite) phases, because the sun also shines light on Earth from different angles.

When the moon appears between Earth and the sun, only its back side—relative to Earth—is illuminated, and we see its dark side, which means we see nothing. This is called the "new moon," for it indicates the beginning of the lunar cycle.

As the moon moves eastward, it "grows." It appears in the western sky at sunset, and its side is illuminated by the sun. This moon is called a "waxing crescent moon." Although only a quarter of it or less is actually lit by the sun, you can usually see the rest of the moon faintly outlined—a crescent moon with a "full moon in its arms." This is caused by sunlight reflecting back to the moon off Earth, and is called "earthshine."

Seven days after the new moon, the moon lies 90 degrees east of the sun. It appears due south for those in the Northern Hemisphere, and due north for those in the Southern Hemisphere. This is called the "first-quarter moon," for one quarter of the moon's surface is visible. A first-quarter moon shines in the eastern sky in late afternoon, rising in broad daylight.

As the moon continues east, it grows in size until it is more rounded in shape, and is then called the "waxing gibbous moon." Again, it rises late iin the afternoon, before the sun sets completely.

About two weeks after the new moon, the sky is lit by the full moon. At this point, the moon lies opposite the sun in the sky. This is the only phase that cannot be seen when the sun is in the sky.

The Moon Illusion

A moon rising in the evening sky appears gigantic. Just a few hours later it shines higher in the sky and seems to be much smaller. But the moon has not really changed size, of course. Instead, the viewer has experienced a simple, natural optical illusion: the moon illusion.

No one really knows what causes the moon illusion, though scientists believe that it has to do with the view of the moon relative to foreground objects. If you look through a loose fist, eliminating the foreground objects from your view, the moon will appear normal-sized again.

A distant horizon will make the rising or setting moon appear larger than it really is. The effect is also noticeable with the sun, constellations, and even airplanes.

After its full phase, the moon moves into a "waning gibbous," and it rises later and later in the evening until it cannot be seen before midnight. Seven days after the full moon, the moon lies 90 degrees from the sun again, except now it is on the opposite side of the sky. It rises around midnight and lies due south for those in the Northern Hemisphere, and at sunrise and due north for those in the Southern Hemisphere. This is known as the "last-quarter moon."

The moon's shape continues to wane, becoming a "waning crescent," and it is visible low in the east only before the sun rises. Finally, the moon disappears completely from the sky once again, as the new moon indicates the new beginning of the lunar phases.

Moon Faces

Chinese legend tells of a man, Wan Ho, who long ago wanted very badly to go to the moon. One night he had his assistants strap him into a chair, strap the chair to a catapult, then place explosives under the chair. When the moon came up they lit the fuses on command, sending Wan Ho and his chair flying into the sky. Since he was never seen again, legend has it that he made it to the moon, and you can see him sitting there, forever strapped in his chair.

This is only one explanation for the many faces and figures that people see when they look at the moon. In ancient times, some people believed that the moon was a beautiful goddess. Others thought it was a giant mirror that reflected the image of our own world. Still others believed the dark shadings were bodies of water.

Today, we have strong telescopes, and astronauts have actually walked on the moon. We know that the dark patches we see on the moon are dry plains of solidified lava, and that the moon does not contain a drop of water. Oddly enough, the dark areas are known as "seas" (which is what they appeared to be to astronomers without benefit of powerful telescopes), such as the Sea of Tranquillity, the Sea of Vapors, the Sea of Foam, and the Sea of Serenity. The surface is also covered with mountains, crevices, and craters.

When you become familiar with the appearance of the moon's face, you will notice that it is always the same. Do not make the mistake of thinking that this means that the moon does not rotate on its own axis. Just the opposite is true. We see the same face on the moon because it rotates at exactly the same rate as it orbits the Earth, thereby always presenting us with the same side. Careful observers will notice that along the edges of the moon, the features may vary slightly. For more information on this, see page 27.

Eclipses

Occasionally the moon passes into the shadow of Earth. This is called a "lunar eclipse," and it occurs only when the moon is full and sits opposite the sun in the sky. Because the moon's orbit is tipped about 5 degrees to the earth-sun plane, lunar eclipses occur only rarely. When they do, the moon can look very strange, sometimes bloodred, and may not completely disappear from view. The red color is due to the effect on the sunlight passing through our atmosphere being

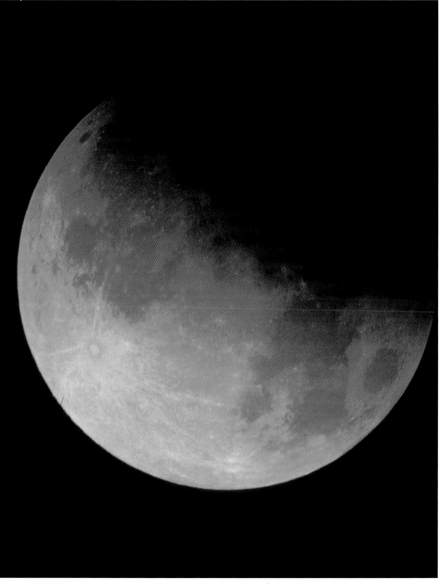

The roundness of Earth's shadow falling on the moon's surface during a lunar eclipse led the ancient Greeks to infer the spherical shape of our planet.

bent inward toward the moon. When the moon moves only partly through Earth's shadow, it is known as a partial lunar eclipse, which is not as dramatic as a total lunar eclipse.

When the moon is new and lies between Earth and the sun, it occasionally blocks the sun from view, causing an eclipse of the sun. *Such eclipses are very dangerous to view and must be watched only indirectly or with proper filtration.*

Total solar eclipses occur when the moon passes directly in front of the sun, thus totally blocking its light and revealing the sun's pearly white atmosphere, referred to as the corona. This occurs only because the moon—smaller but closer—and the sun—bigger but farther away—appear the same size, about half a degree across. Partial eclipses occur when the moon only partially blocks the sun's light; they can be watched with the aid of a pinhole projector. *As at any time, it is not safe to look directly at the sun or partial solar eclipses.*

The sun should never *be observed directly.*

A Pinhole Projector

Using a sewing needle or a paper clip, prick a tiny hole in a thick piece of cardboard. Hold the cardboard up to the sunlight, then hold a sheet of white paper several inches below it. You will see the image of the solar eclipse projected onto the paper. This is a safe way to view a partial solar eclipse. A total eclipse—where the corona is visible—is perfectly safe to view directly without fear.

Because the moon does not travel around Earth in a perfect circle, it sometimes lies farther from our planet than at other times and appears a bit smaller than the sun. If the moon moves in front of the sun at this time, you may see an annular eclipse, which is when a ring, or "annulus," of sunlight is still able to shine through.

An Up-Close View

It is so easy just to look up in the sky and see the moon that some people don't think to take a closer look. The moon, with all its nooks and crannies, "seas," and craters, is a terrific specimen for close observation. In fact, examining its detail can be just as fascinating as searching the heavens for a distant star.

Many people believe that the best time to look at the moon is when it is in its full phase. Actually, nothing could be further from the truth. You need shadows and contrasts to make out the details of the moon, and when the sun is shining fully on the moon, these shadows are virtually nonexistent and the surface appears flat and dull.

It is fascinating to observe the moon during its different phases. During the thin crescent phase, you will see the darkened surface of earthshine. The gibbous phase is the best time to study the lunar maria, or "seas." The very best time to view lunar craters and mountains, however, is during the thick crescent and quarter phases. At this time, sunlight falls at a steep angle on the craters, mountains, valleys, and rills, and creates long shadows along the "terminator," the boundary between lunar night and day. If you study this area every night, you will see that the features there seem to change every day. That is because as the moon orbits, the sun shines on it at slightly different angles. As the angle changes, new features become visible to us on Earth.

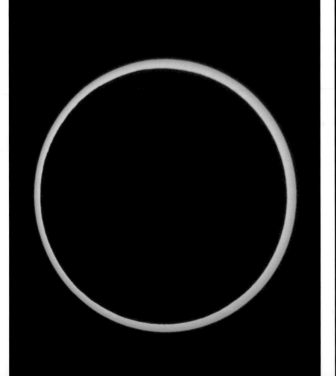

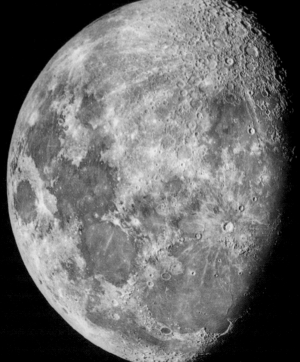

Far left: A solar eclipse that occurs when the moon is farther—and the sun closer—than normal creates an annular eclipse. Left: The best time to view the moon with a telescope is when the sunrise or sunset line—the "terminator"—creates stark shadows of craters and mountains.

A spacecraft orbiting the moon would show that the moon's far side appears significantly different than its Earth-facing side.

Features of the Moon

Take a tour of the moon with a simple backyard telescope and a good lunar map, and you will quickly become familiar with its myriad features and terrains. There are the colorfully named lunar maria, such as the Lake of the Dead and the Ocean of Storms. These dried lava planes are relic effects from the moon's formative stages. In fact, nearly a third of the moon's surface is covered with remnant lava flows.

Around the edges of the maria, you will see long mountain ranges. Most of these are named after mountain ranges on Earth, though many are much taller. Some are as much as 4 miles (6.4km) high.

All over the lunar surface, you will also find deep cracks, rills, and valleys. And craters abound on the moon's surface; some are even craters within craters. They range in diameter from a few miles to as long as 150 miles (240km) across.

Because the moon rotates on its axis at the same speed as it orbits the Earth, it would seem that we always see the same side of the moon. This is not quite true. The moon's orbit around Earth is not a perfect circle, and Earth does not sit exactly in the middle of the moon's orbit. Therefore, the moon's speed is not constant, but it moves more quickly when it is at its perigee than at its apogee. As a result, if you observe the moon regularly, it is possible to peek around its eastern and western limbs about every two weeks. You can also see the northern and southern edges, for the moon's orbit around Earth is tipped at about 5 degrees. This combination of circumstances actually allows us to see up to 59 percent of the moon's surface over time. The moon's far side, however, remains invisible to those watching from Earth.

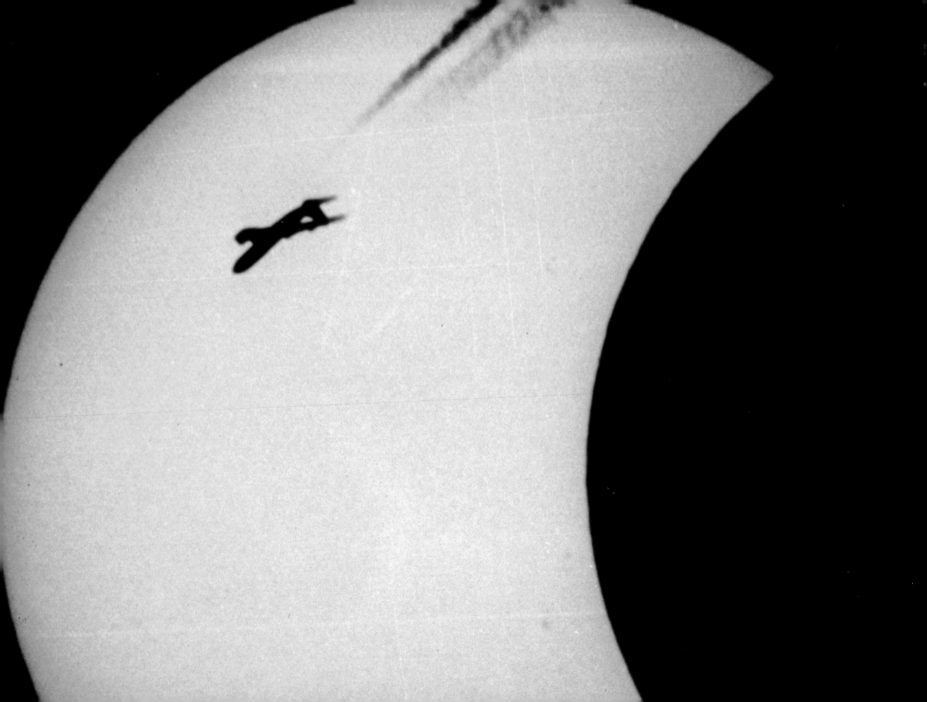

Chapter *3*

The Source of Life – the Sun

The sun is the nearest—and most familiar—star. A body made mostly of hydrogen gases, it has a surface temperature of some 10,000°F (5,500°C). It burns not by fire, but by nuclear fusion. Deep in its core, where temperatures exceed 10 million °F (5.5 million °C), hydrogen atoms speed around, slamming into one another so hard that they fuse and form helium. In the process, they release energy in the form of light and heat. Eventually, that energy works its way out of the sun and radiates into space. Some of this energy warms our world, making life on our planet possible.

The sun is so huge that a million Earths could fit inside it, and a hundred Earths lined up side by side would not reach across its diameter, which is 864,400 miles (1,383,000km). Compared to other stars, however, our sun is quite average in size and temperature. Very small stars are thought to have diameters of only 4,000 miles (6,400km), while the largest stars are estimated to have diameters 3,000 times that of the sun.

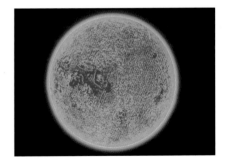

*Left: The moon's silhouette can be seen against the sun during a partial solar eclipse. A passing airliner creates its own solar eclipse. **Above, top:** The sun's outer atmosphere, the corona, stretches past Earth and may affect our planet. **Above, bottom:** The sun's inner atmosphere, the photosphere, is what we see every day.*

What's New Under the Sun?

Because the sun is our closest star and the source of life on Earth, it is fascinating to us. Even though it does not shine at night, the sun is still an exciting specimen for the beginning astronomer. It is constantly changing and exhibiting interesting phenomena.

The first thing you will discover when looking at the sun in a safe manner is that it has sunspots—dark markings that appear around its face. No one knows precisely what sunspots are, but scientists believe they are cooler areas of the sun's atmosphere that occur in the regions of magnetic storms.

Most sunspots are many times larger than Earth. They are not static, but change from day to day and week to week. Some grow in size, while others break up and disappear. Over time, you will notice that they seem to march across the sun's face. This occurs because the sun itself is rotating. Sunspots at the edges of the sun's surface appear elongated, while the ones at the center do not. That is because you are viewing them from a different perspective. Those on the edge are carried by the sun's ro-

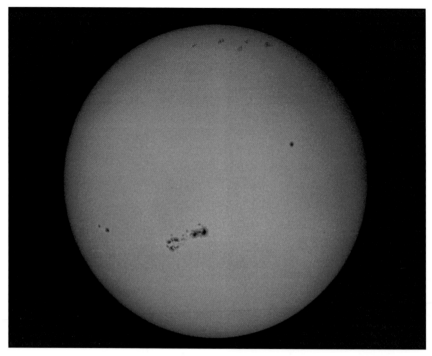

tation from or toward the back side of the solar disk, or are turning toward or away from you, the viewer. This makes them look distorted.

The number of sunspots changes constantly. In fact, their numbers increase and decrease over a cycle of approximately 11 years, a period known as the "sunspot cycle."

The sun's limbs appear slightly darker and redder than the middle of the sun's disk. This is known as "limb-

darkening," and it occurs because the sun is a sphere of gas whose energy-producing region is near its center. The limb is away from that center and produces no energy, so it is natural that it appears darker than the center.

Bright, irregular patches near the sun's limb are called "faculae." Faculae are hot gases rising to the top of the sun's atmosphere. They are most visible at the solar limb, for the contrast is greater there than at the disk's center.

The sun is a fascinating object to view, but extreme care must be taken before aiming a telescope in its direction.

Safety First!

The sun is extremely dangerous to observe. Never look directly at the sun with the naked eye, binoculars, or a telescope. Its intense visible light and its invisible ultraviolet and infrared radiations need only an instant to burn the retina and cause blindness. Even during a partial solar eclipse, so much radiation is emitted that blindness can result instantly.

Sun filters that attach to your telescope's eyepiece are extremely dangerous and must never be used. If your telescope comes with such a device, destroy it immediately. For safe ways to view the sun, refer to the discussion on page 32.

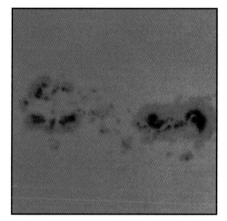

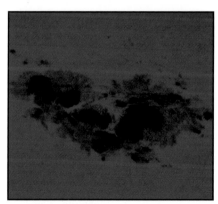

Above, top and bottom: Sunspots provide exciting and constantly changing features on the otherwise bland disk of the sun. ***Right:*** The turbulence of the sun's atmosphere can be seen only through specialized filters.

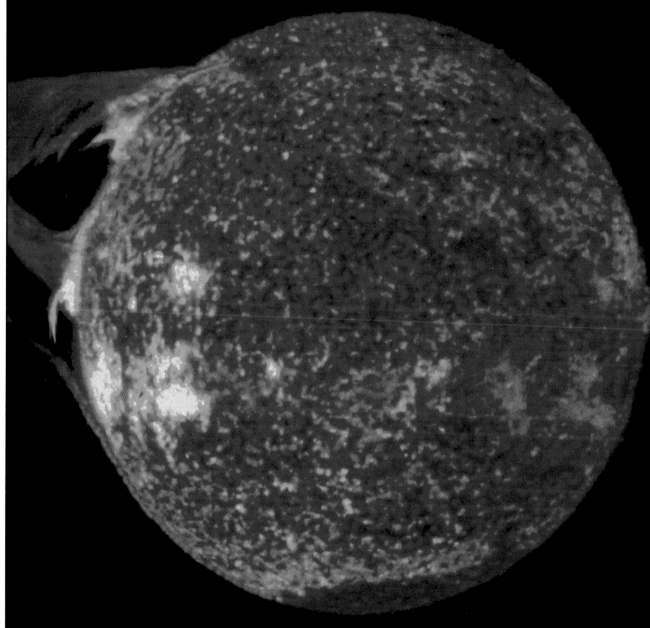

Another feature of the sun is granulation. Huge convection cells, or bubbles, transport heat from below the sun's visible disk out into space; these appear as bright specks on the sun. Conversely, the sun's cooler gases move downward, and these appear as darker specks. These convection cells give the sun a lemon-peel appearance that is visible on a good, clear morning. However, they are extremely small and of low contrast, and can be seen only during excellent conditions and with powerful telescopes.

Safe Viewing

The safest way to view the phenomena of the sun is indirectly. The method for watching an eclipse described on page 25 is an indirect method. The best way to view the sun indirectly with a telescope is with eyepiece projection.

To create eyepiece projection, set up your telescope and let its temperature adjust to that of the outdoors, which should take about half an hour. Now, aim the instrument toward the sun, *but not by looking through it or the*

Solar projection not only provides the safest way to view the sun; it also allows groups to enjoy the view with you.

finderscope. (In fact, it is probably a good idea to remove the finderscope completely or cover its objective end to prevent a disastrous mistake.) Instead, watch the shadow the telescope tube makes on the ground until it changes from an elongated oval to a circle. That means sunlight is streaming directly down the tube.

Now, hold a piece of white cardboard behind the eyepiece. You should see the sun's disk projected onto it. If you don't, you need to adjust the telescope slightly. *Remember not to do this by looking through the telescope.* When the sun's image comes into view on the cardboard, turn the focusing knobs until the projected image is sharp. Turn

the telescope away or cover it every few minutes to avoid heat buildup inside its tube.

For even better viewing, enclose your white projection screen in a partially closed cardboard box painted black on the inside. This will reduce the scattered light on the screen and increase the sharpness and contrast of the solar image while still allowing you and others to view the sun safely.

There are solar filters on the market that allow direct viewing of the sun. They are expensive, and they must be used with care. Do not consider any filter that is placed on the eyepiece, but only those that are placed between the instrument and the sun. Use any of these filters with extreme caution, following the directions carefully and thoroughly.

✳

The sun is the center of our solar system, a dynamic and ever-changing ball of energy that fuels life as we know it. It is a fascinating specimen to study, as long as you remember its power and the vital importance of viewing it with extreme caution.

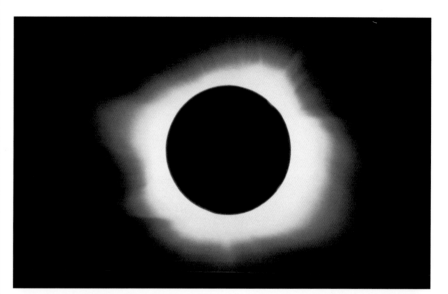

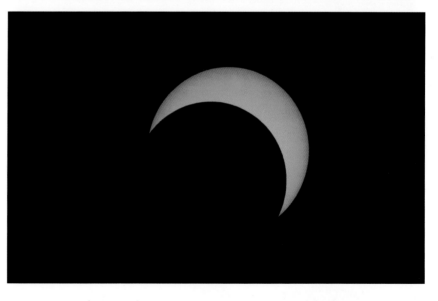

Above: *Solar eclipses are spectacles that always attract a crowd, and they offer an excellent opportunity to use solar projection.* **Right, top:** *The solar corona, the sun's pearly-white atmosphere, can be seen only during a total solar eclipse.* **Right, bottom:** *A major partial eclipse can cause the sky to darken so much that animals think it's dusk.*

Chapter 4

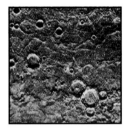

Our Neighbors— the Planets

Some of the most exciting astronomical subjects are the planets. To observe them with any real detail, you need a telescope, a good viewing spot, terrific conditions, and lots of patience.

A good look at the planets reveals that they are not really points of light, but disks. They do not stay in one place, but move through the stars with regularity and predictability. They normally move eastward, but will occasionally travel west during times of opposition.

When you turn your telescope on a planet, you will notice that it seems to waver slightly. This is because of atmospheric turbulence, the same condition that makes the stars twinkle. However, it does not affect the planets as much, because the planets are disks, not points of light.

The key to seeing the fine details of the planets is to use high magnifications and carefully watch a planet's disk as the air moves around in front of it. Occasionally, the turbulence will steady for an instant or so, which will provide you with a spectacularly clear, sharp image of the planet.

The inner planets—Mercury and Venus—lie closer to the sun than Earth does and always appear in the sun's direction. Therefore, they can be seen only at dusk and dawn.

The rest of the planets—excluding Earth, of course—are all farther away from the sun than Earth is, and for that reason can be seen at any time of night and often appear very high in the sky. In addition, we see them only in their

*Left: The surface of cloud-covered Venus was first unveiled by radar imaging from the orbiting Magellan spacecraft. **Above:** This is the region of the planet Mercury known as Caloris Basin, revealed by spacecraft photography.*

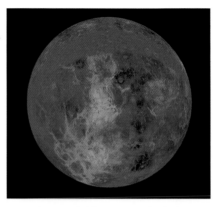

gibbous and full phases. The best time to observe them is when they are in opposition to the sun, when Earth and the planet are closest together. Most of the outer planets are large and produce spectacular images, even when seen through a small telescope.

Mercury

Average distance from the sun: 36 million miles (58 million km)

Equatorial diameter: 3,023 miles (4,837km)

Period of revolution: 0.24 Earth years

Daytime temperature: 600°F (316°C)

Discovery: Known since ancient times

Notable features: Occasional phases

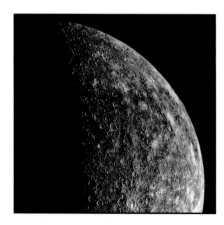

Mercury can be seen only at dawn and dusk, for it lies closer to the sun than the Earth does and always appears in the sun's direction. It is the most elusive of the planets because it is so small and so distant, often more than 90 million miles (144 million km) from Earth. Also, because it lies so close to the sun and can be seen only near the horizon, where atmospheric turbulence or wavering is the greatest, viewers rarely see it with any detail.

Venus

Average distance from the sun: 67 million miles (107 million km)

Equatorial diameter: 7,504 miles (12,006km)

Period of revolution: 0.62 Earth years

Daytime temperature: 867°F (464°C)

Discovery: Known since ancient times

Notable features: Cloud-covered, occasional phases

Like Mercury, Venus, the other planet between Earth and the sun, can be seen only at dusk and dawn. Unlike Mercury, Venus is very interesting to watch. Venus moves higher in the sky and is

sometimes visible in total darkness, hours after sunset and before sunrise. It is best to observe Venus when it is highest in the sky.

Venus is about the same size and mass as Earth, but it is covered by clouds of carbon dioxide and carbon monoxide, so surface features are obscured. However, these white clouds make it sparkle brilliantly in the dawn or dusk because they reflect nearly all the sunlight that hits them.

Watching Venus on a regular basis, you will notice that it shows phases like those of the moon. When the planet lies on the opposite side of the sun, at its most distant point from Earth, it is in the position of "superior conjunction" and appears as a tiny full disk. As Venus swings around the sun, however, sunlight falls on it from different angles, and it seems to grow in size and also changes its phase. As it ap-

proaches its position between the sun and Earth—known as "inferior conjunction"—Venus appears as a large, thin crescent.

Earth

Average distance from the sun: 93 million miles (149 million km)

Equatorial diameter: 9,654 miles (15,446km)

Period of revolution: 1 Earth year

Daytime temperature: 60°F (16°C)

Discovery: Known since ancient times

Notable features: Blue oceans, white clouds

Mars

Average distance from the sun: 137 million miles (219 million km)

Equatorial diameter: 4,072 miles (6,515km)

Period of revolution: 1.88 Earth years

Daytime temperature: 50°F (10°C)

Discovery: Known since ancient times

Notable features: Orange surface, dark markings, white polar caps

Unlike many of the other outer planets, Mars is barely half the size of Earth.

Above: *Photographed from space by the Apollo 17 astronauts, Earth shows its distinctive blue oceans, white clouds and ice caps, and green and brown land masses.*
Right: *Though Mars is smaller than Earth, spacecraft photos show a gaping chasm that would stretch from San Francisco to New York City.*

Therefore, it is difficult to see much detail on Mars with a small telescope. It is easiest to see when it is at or near opposition. At these times, when it is closest to Earth, it shines more than 50 times brighter than when it is farthest away.

To the naked eye, Mars looks like a reddish orange light shining in the heavens. A telescope reveals one or two white ice caps at its poles and dark markings across its face. Stronger telescopes show that Mars is a patchwork of red, gray, and white. Scientists believe that the red areas, which cover more than 60 percent of the planet's surface, are deserts. The gray areas, which cover about 40 percent, change from gray in the Martian winter to blue-gray in the summer. The white patches are poles; their size also changes with the seasons—larger in winter, smaller in summer.

Mars rotates on its axis every 24 hours, so you can watch its progress during the course of the night. It also has two moons, which are so small that they are impossible to see except through a very strong telescope. Named Phobos (fear) and Deimos (panic) for the two mythological companions of Mars, the god of war, they are only 10 miles (16km) and 7 miles (11km) in diameter, respectively. Phobos is only 5,800 miles (9,280km) from the center of Mars and 3,700 miles (5,920km) from its surface. Its orbit around Mars takes only 7 hours and 39 minutes, and it rises and sets in 4½ hours. Deimos is 14,600 miles (23,360km) from Mars' center and 12,500 miles (20,000km) from its surface, and revolves around the planet in 30 hours and 18 minutes.

Jupiter

Average distance from the sun: 467
  million miles (747 million km)
Equatorial diameter: 85,680 miles
  (137,088km)
Period of revolution: 11.86 Earth years
Daytime temperature: -184°F (-120°C)
Discovery: Known since ancient times
Notable features: Colorful cloud bands,
  Great Red Spot, four bright moons

Jupiter is 11 times larger than Earth and is therefore one of the most spectacular specimens for the small telescope. In fact, because the planet rotates so rapidly—9 hours, 50 minutes, and 30 seconds—it is possible to see all sides of Jupiter in one long night of observation.

To the naked eye, Jupiter appears as a bright yellowish object. With the aid of a telescope, you can see its colorful cloud bands and its four moons. You will also notice that it is not perfectly round, but slightly flattened. This is because of its rapid rotation, which causes its gaseous atmosphere to flatten. You will also see the Great Red Spot, which is actually a gigantic hurricane some 3 times larger than Earth. It is seen as a rose-colored marking among the clouds of Jupiter.

Jupiter is known to have sixteen moons, the four largest of which are the easiest and most interesting to observe. They appear as bright stars that lie in a nearly straight line across the planet's equatorial region. They are known as the Galilean moons because Galileo discovered them in 1610. The innermost moon is known as Io, and it shines with a slightly orange color. Next is Europa, then Ganymede, and the outermost is Callisto. If you watch these moons closely from night to night, you will discover how they move as they orbit Jupiter. With a more powerful telescope, you can watch them move into the planet's giant shadow and disappear for a while in an eclipse. You can also watch them pass in front of the planet and cast their own shadows across its clouds.

Saturn

Average distance from the sun: 854
  million miles (1.3 billion km)
Equatorial diameter: 75,100 miles
  (120,160km)
Period of revolution: 29.46 Earth years
Daytime temperature: -291°F (-179°C)
Discovery: Known since ancient times
Notable features: Ring system

Although Saturn appears to be a dull yellow to the unaided eye, it is at times one of the brightest objects in the sky. At its brightest, it shines at just less than 0 magnitude, while at its faintest it is around 1st magnitude. This is amazing, considering that it is about 1 billion miles (1.6 billion km) from Jupiter.

However, Saturn's most fascinating feature is its rings. They are about 2½ times larger than its body and quite easy to see through a low-powered telescope. Although the rings appear solid,

Left: The giant planet Jupiter's atmosphere is mottled with turbulent weather systems, including the Great Red Spot, which is three times larger than Earth. Above: The Voyager 2 *spacecraft revealed a marvelously complex ring system surrounding the planet Saturn.*

they are really made up of billions of chunks of rock and ice whirling at tens of thousands of miles per hour. This will be evident to you after some observation, as you can occasionally see a star shining through the rings.

Unfortunately, our view of Saturn's rings changes every 15 years or so, because the rings are tipped about 27 degrees to our line of sight. Sometimes, as in 1988, we get the best possible view of the rings. At other times, such as in 1995, the rings turn edge-on and disappear completely. They will slowly come back into view and will reach their maximum tilt again in 2003.

Our first view of a "crescent" Uranus came in 1986, courtesy of Voyager 2.

Uranus

Average distance from the sun: 1,720
   million miles (2,752 million km)
Equatorial diameter: 30,720 miles
   (49,152km)
Period of revolution: 84.01 Earth years
Daytime temperature: -344°F (-209°C)
Discovery: Herschel, 1781
Notable features: None

Uranus lies about 2 billion miles from the sun and is very faint in our sky. In fact, it is generally not visible to the naked eye, and even with a telescope, very little detail is revealed. Everything that we know about this planet comes courtesy of the *Voyager 2* spacecraft. For instance, it is now known that Uranus has an atmos-phere primarily of hydrogen, methane, and ammonia; the methane gives it its blue-green cast. It does have a system of rings and satellites. Other than that, the *Voyager 2* revealed very few significant features. It takes Uranus and its fifteen moons 84 years to complete one revolution around the sun.

Neptune

Average distance from the sun:
   2,693 million miles (4.3 billion km)
Equatorial diameter: 29,160 miles
   (46,656km)
Period of revolution: 164.79 Earth years
Daytime temperature: -357°F (-216°C)
Discovery: Adams and Leverrier, 1846
Notable features: Dark and bright spots

Nearly the same size as Uranus, Neptune appears in a strong telescope as a bluish green disk with an 8th-magnitude brightness. It is almost 3 billion miles (4.8 billion km) from the sun and takes 165 years to orbit. Neptune was shown by the *Voyager 2* to be similar in composition to Uranus but with visible clouds and storm systems in its atmosphere and some identifiable features. They include the Great Dark Spot (a huge storm system in the planet's southern hemisphere) and the Bright Companion (a cloud formation that is associated with the Dark Spot).

Pluto

Average distance from the sun:

   3,544 million miles (5.6 billion km)

Equatorial diameter: 1,380 miles

   (2,208km)

Period of revolution: 247.69 Earth years

Daytime temperature: -396°F (-237°C)

Discovery: Tombaugh, 1930

Notable features: None

The sun shines 900 times fainter on Pluto than it does on Earth. Pluto has a moon named Charon, which is 60 times larger than Earth's moon. This moon never sets or rises, but is locked in the same position above the horizon of the planet. At an average distance from the sun of 3.6 billion miles (5.7 billion km), Pluto takes almost 248 years to make one revolution around its distant light source. It actually has an eccentric orbit that at times brings it closer than Neptune to the sun. It is currently in that position, having crossed into the orbit of Neptune in 1979, and will remain there until 1999.

✳

Like members of a family, each of the planets displays similar behavior to the other planets, yet with a unique personality that shines through. As you become familiar with the patterns of the planets, you will be favored with a glimpse of their distinct characteristics. But remember, as you learn about our eight neighbors that they are only a tiny group among the myriad stars and galaxies in existence.

Above, left: Scientists were shocked when Voyager 2 *revealed Neptune in 1989 as a complex and colorful world.* **Above, right:** *The sun would appear as a bright star in the nighttime sky from Pluto and its moon, Charon, as shown in this artist's conception.*

Chapter *5*

Deeper in the Sky

Beyond the moon, beyond the planets, and beyond the sun shine millions and millions of stars. On a clear night, you can see thousands of them with just the naked eye. However, with the aid of a telescope, good viewing conditions, a detailed star map, and a lot of patience, you will be amazed at the wonderful things you will find deeper in the sky.

The Milky Way

The most familiar feature of the "Great Beyond" is, of course, the Milky Way, the great galactic structure of which our tiny solar system is a part. We are able to see the Milky Way because our sun is positioned two-thirds of the way out from its center. To the naked eye, the Milky Way appears as a hazy band of light that streams overhead. But if you gaze along this band with binoculars or a small telescope, you will discover that it is made up of millions of stars that stretch for trillions of miles.

Observers in the Northern Hemisphere get some of their best views of the Milky Way in the direction of the constellation Cygnus, the Swan. Those south of Earth's equator will find the viewing spectacular toward the constellation of Sagittarius.

Deep-Sky Objects

With a fairly powerful telescope (greater than 3 inches [7.6cm] in diameter), you will be able to see dozens of

*Left: The Milky Way is home to 400 billion stars, star clusters, and interstellar clouds of gas and dust, and forms a magnificent sight on dark nights. **Above:** Around our Milky Way Galaxy are about 120 globular star clusters, such as M22 in the constellation Sagittarius.*

The Eta Carinae Nebula forms one of the most popular deep-sky objects in the heavens.

deep-sky objects such as open or globular clusters of stars, diffuse or planetary nebulae, and spiral or elliptical galaxies. They are extremely far from Earth, faint, and very difficult to find, so you may be frustrated at first. When you *do* find them, your struggle will have been worth it, for they are some of the most beautiful and majestic sights in the heavens.

The Great Orion Nebula, found in the "sword" of Orion, the Hunter, is one of the most prolific star-forming regions in our galaxy and is a treat for those with small telescopes.

Messier's List

It is best to begin searching the deep sky for the objects on Messier's list. These items are known not only by their proper names but by a code number that begins with "M," such as M42, which is the Orion Nebula.

How these objects came to be cataloged in Messier's list is an interesting story. An eighteenth-century astronomer, Charles Messier, spent his career searching the heavens for comets, which he knew would first appear as faint, fuzzy blotches, then move among the stars over a period of several nights. Every time Messier located one of these hazy blotches, he made note of it and watched it carefully for motion. More often than not, the object never moved but appeared fixed to the starry vault. Messier became so frustrated with all his false comet discoveries that he began to compile a list of these objects so that other astronomers would not mistake them for comets as he had done.

Ironically, it is his list of 103 "nuisances," not comets, for which Messier is known today. Published in 1784, this famous list is known as the Messier Catalog, and because Messier used only a small telescope, it is an excellent place for beginners to find deep-space objects they can observe without too much frustration.

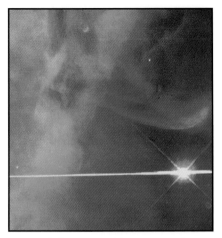  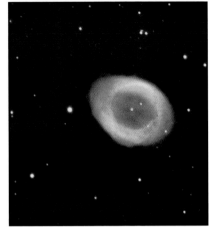

*Above, left: The Hubble Space Telescope has revealed the dark knot at the top of this frame—direct evidence of stars and planets that are forming in the Orion Nebula. **Above, middle:** Dark clouds, such as the famous Horsehead Nebula, are the thick sites of star formation in our galaxy. **Above, right:** When stars age and die, they lose their outer atmospheres, such as this example known as the Ring Nebula in Lyra.*

Interstellar Clouds or Nebulae

Located just below the belt of Orion, the Hunter, is the Orion Nebula (M42), one of the most spectacular deep-sky objects in the heavens. Visible to the naked eye, it is best observed in winter in the Northern Hemisphere and in summer in the Southern Hemisphere.

Nebulae are clouds of gas and dust within our galaxy. Most are dark, but some are illuminated by nearby stars or stars embedded in them. If you look at the Orion Nebula with a small telescope, you will see wisps of luminous gas and dust stretching across your entire field of vision. At the nebula's center lies a cluster of four bluish white stars known as the Trapezium. These stars illuminate the nebula from within, making it visible to us 1,500 light-years away.

The Orion Nebula is one of the most prolific star-forming regions in our galaxy. Among its clouds, clumps of material are collapsing under their own weight. When their internal temperatures rise high enough to begin nuclear fusion, they ignite and shine brightly across space. As fascinating and dramatic as this process is, it takes hundreds of thousands or even millions of years to occur, so don't expect to see it in your telescope.

There are many nebulae in the galaxy, some star-producing, others the remnants of stellar death. The Ring Nebula (M57), located 2,300 light-years away in the direction of the constellation Lyra, the Harp, is one such nebula. In a small telescope, it appears as a tiny gray smoke ring among the stars. This "ring" is actually a shell that was blown off a star in its final gasp of life ages ago. The star itself—visible right at the center of the ring, but only in a large telescope—is believed to have once been much like our sun. If any life had originated and evolved on planets near this star, it is most certainly gone now.

Astronomers believe that our sun will react as this ancient star did so many years ago, when it, too, exhausts its supply of hydrogen fuel—some 5 billion years in the future.

Star Clusters and Spiral Galaxies

One of the most famous star clusters of all is the Pleiades (M45), located in Taurus, the Bull. This grouping of stars is also known as the Seven Sisters because some observers can see seven of its stars without optical aid. When viewed through even a small telescope, this cluster bursts into dozens of stars. Most are young, hot, bluish stars that, on a clear, dark night, seem to sparkle like proverbial diamonds in the sky. Pleiades is an "open" cluster, which means its stars are bound loosely by mutual gravitation.

Not all clusters are open. In the direction of the constellation of Hercules shines a distant cluster of thousands of stars so compact that it appears as a globe of stars. Hence, it is known as the Globular Cluster in Hercules (M13). Only a hundred or so globular clusters are known to astronomers. These stars appear to form the halo around the center of our Milky Way Galaxy, which is located behind the constellation of Sagittarius. Stronger telescopes are needed to distinguish individual stars, but these globes are quite spectacular even in small instruments.

The Andromeda Galaxy (M31) is a spiral galaxy similar to but larger than the Milky Way, and is visible on autumn and winter evenings in the Northern Hemisphere (spring and summer evenings in the Southern Hemisphere). To the naked eye, it looks like an elongated blob of light. When viewed with a telescope, it appears as an even larger, hazy, elliptical blob. What you are actually seeing is only the central region of the galaxy. The outlying areas, where the spiral pattern lies, are much too faint to see except with powerful telescopes.

It is astonishing to realize that the Andromeda Galaxy is the most distant object we can see with the naked eye. Located 2 million light-years away, its light was given off long before humans walked on Earth.

Southern Hemisphere observers have the privilege of being able to see two more galaxies: the Large and Small Magellanic Clouds (LMC and SMC). The

Above: One of the most beautiful star clusters in our galaxy is known as the Pleiades, or the Seven Sisters, believed by some astronomers to be a relatively young cluster. **Right:** The nearest galaxy to our Milky Way, the Large Magellanic Cloud, is a spectacular sight under a dark sky south of the equator.

LMC and SMC are actually galaxies near the Milky Way and appear as two amorphous patches of light among the stars of the Southern Hemisphere. They are indeed distant galaxies, though not as distant as the Andromeda Galaxy: the LMC and SMC lie 163,000 and 196,000 light-years away, respectively.

✳

These are only a few of the many amazing deep-sky sights that can be observed by the backyard astronomer armed with a small telescope, a dark sky, a good star map, and a good supply of patience. Although exploration can be frustrating at first for the beginner, the discoveries that are sure to follow make it all worthwhile.

Chapter

Stargazing Essentials

There are so many wondrous things to look at in the sky that you probably can't wait to get out there and start observing. However, there are a few things you need to consider, or you are going to meet with frustration right away. Deep stargazing requires the best possible conditions: ideally, a remote location with no city lights, no moon, and a clear sky. Of course, this best-of-all-possible stargazing scenarios cannot be yours every night. Even so, on just about any night—if you keep your expectations flexible—you will find something fascinating to watch.

Lucky is the astronomer who finds a site high on the top of a remote (but accessible!) mountain, where the sky is unadulterated by city lights and free from bad weather. Of course, as soon as one astronomer finds such a place, hundreds of others will flock there.

Most backyard stargazers encounter conditions that don't begin to approach that, yet they manage to be astounded almost every night by the things they discover. How do they do it? They simply evaluate the conditions they have and adjust their observations and expectations accordingly. They don't expect to look into deep space on a night when there are clouds, but instead concentrateon studying the planets or maybe the moon. They make the best of the opportunity afforded by a clear, moonless night to look far beyond, to the phenomena many, many light-years away.

*Left: Few sights are more stunning than a beautiful full moon rising in the east at dusk. **Above:** The early evening sky can provide many fascinating sights, such as Jupiter, for those who spend time outdoors.*

Above, left: Begin your observing as the sky darkens, whether you're observing with your eyes, binoculars, or a telescope. Above, right: Conjunctions between planets and the moon can provide a unique three-dimensional perspective on the solar system.

Site Conditions

When you are just beginning to learn your way around the sky, you will get enormous pleasure and challenge from watching from your own backyard. In fact, a city site is actually an excellent place from which to begin, because from there one can see only the brightest, most obvious stars.

With a little experience, it won't be long before you will desire a more open, unadulterated view. City lights shine from street lamps, houses, shopping centers, parking lots, and other places. All serve to brighten the night, which is good for city dwellers who need to get about, but terrible for astronomers. A desirable site gives you a clear view of a good deal of the sky, not just a sliver between your house and the folks next door and is far away from light pollution.

Sky Conditions

Even if you find the best possible observation site, you should take into account a number of nightly conditions in order to spend your observation time looking for the things you are most likely to see well. First of all, the best nights for viewing are those when there is no moon. The moon's light, though very beautiful, washes the faint stars and constellations from view. It would not be worth your effort to trek to your dark-sky observation point on a night when the moon is filling the sky with light. On such a night, concentrate instead on watching the brighter stars, planets, and constellations.

A City View

The sky of December through March has the brightest stars, so this is probably the best time to start observing if your location is in the city. You can start to learn by locating Orion, with its three-star belt, and Betelgeuse, the red star that sits on Orion's right shoulder. You will also be able to identify Rigel, the bright, bluish white star at Orion's left thigh. In Canis Major, Orion's Big Dog, you will be able to locate Sirius, the night's brightest star. Seeing all these is not a bad night's work for a view from the city.

The second factor to consider when planning your night's session is the "transparency" of the sky. Degrees of transparency are decided by the amount of clouds or haze in the sky, which can obscure the view on an otherwise perfect night. Remember that after the sun has set, it is sometimes difficult to evaluate how much cloud cover there is in the sky, and this cloud cover will affect what you can see. Try to check out the cloud conditions before the sun sets.

Finally, you will need to determine the amount of twinkling, called "scintillation," in the sky. Scintillation is when the light from a star is bounced around by air currents, making it appear to waver and twinkle. Although scintillation is pretty to watch, it is devastating to stargazers because it obscures detail.

The measure of the atmosphere's steadiness is called "seeing." To measure seeing, find a bright star high overhead. If it twinkles noticeably, the seeing is bad. If it shines with a steady light, the seeing is good. A measure of seeing determines, in part, how faint an object you will be able to see and how much fine detail will be visible in the sky.

Left: The Big Dipper appears in the Northern Hemisphere sky, revolving constantly around Polaris, the North Star. Below: The plane of the Milky Way stretches across the sky from horizon to horizon, creating an impressive sight from a dark location.

If you experience a moonless, cloudless night when the seeing is excellent or good, explore some of the fainter and harder-to-see parts of the sky. If the seeing is fair or poor, concentrate on brighter features in the sky.

Being aware of the conditions that will affect your night's viewing will make it more rewarding for you. If you spend a whole session looking for a deep-space object on a night when it could not be clearly seen with even a powerful telescope, you will quickly give up on stargazing. Instead, plan ahead, watching the sky as evening sets in and assessing the conditions, and remain flexible, altering your observing plans according to the qualities of the sky on that particular night.

Chapter 7

Stargazing Tools and Techniques

Unlike cats, who see well in the dark, people do their best seeing during the day when there is a lot of light. Scientists and doctors, who want to see things up close and as sharp as possible, add even more light to daylight to aid in their viewing. Shining light on something brings out more detail and helps you to see it.

Stargazers, who observe their subjects at night, seem to have chosen the worst possible time for the human eye to try to see anything with much detail. Furthermore, they can't shine more light on their subjects; they are just too far away. Instead, they use a few tools and techniques to help them see into the dark sky, including telescopes and star maps, as well as night vision and averted vision.

Night Vision

Whenever you move suddenly from a bright situation to a dark one, such as walking into a dark movie theater after being outdoors in the sunshine, for a little while it seems even darker than it really is. This is because your eyes are accustomed to bright sunlight, and under those conditions pupils do not have to be open very wide to get the light they need for the eyes to see well. Once you have been in the theater for some time, your eyes adjust to the dark, that is, your pupils open wider in order to take in all the light they can. Now with your pupils dilated, you look around the theater wondering why you ever had a hard time seeing your way around at first.

Left: Telescopes of many different types and sizes are available to enhance your viewing pleasure. Above: An observer may use either a small finderscope or a coordinate dial to find faint objects more easily.

Stargazers have the same problem when they move from a lighted area to their observation site. At first they can't see many of the stars because their eyes are used to seeing in more light. Gradually, however, their eyes become adapted, and they can see the fainter stars in the sky above.

It takes about 10 to 30 minutes for your eyes to adjust to the dark, and you should make sure they are adjusted before you begin your stargazing session. One way to do this is to sit in a dark room before you begin your observing session. Another way is to go outdoors early, before it is dark, and let your eyes become adapted at your site.

Once your eyes are adjusted to the dark and are seeing as well as they can, you must preserve this dark adaptation by avoiding any bright or white light. But how can you keep records or look at your star map in the dark? Astronomers use red light, which protects dark-adapted eyes, to complete these tasks at the site. You can make a red light by covering your flashlight with red cellophane or by painting the bulb with red nail polish. With a red light,

you can see everything around you without hampering your night vision.

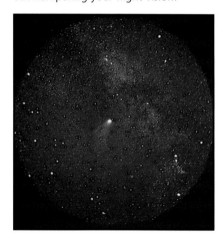

Some celestial objects are so faint—like the tail of Halley's Comet—that the only way we can see them is with averted vision.

Averted Vision

Even when your eyes are adapted to the darkness, you can't see as well at night as you can during the day. For that reason, it's a good idea to make sure that you are looking at the things you want to see as efficiently as possible. Seasoned astronomers know that the best way to see faint objects at night is with averted vision.

The premise behind averted vision is that you can see faint objects better with the edges of the retina than with the center. The central part of the retina contains color receptors, known as "cones." Cones perceive color for us, but they need a lot of light to do this. The outer part of the retina contains the black-and-white sensors, known as "rods." These help us see when light is scarce, but do not perceive any color at all.

To see faint detail in the sky, use your rods instead of your cones. Instead of looking directly at a faint object, look at it slightly off to one side. This way you will see the object out of the corner of your eye where the rods are working.

This technique is particularly useful when trying to observe very faint celestial bodies, whether with the naked eye or through a telescope. Remember that seeing with the rods of your eyes means that you are not seeing color, so everything you look at will appear to be a greenish gray. However, the thrill of seeing these distant phenomena will make up for their lack of hue.

Telescope Techniques

When you use a telescope to look even closer at and deeper into the night sky, you will want to make sure that you are getting the best from your instrument and your eyes. Here are some astronomical tricks-of-the-trade that should help you along.

✳ Preserve your night vision. Resist the temptation to use anything other than your red light to see your notes or read your star map. Avoid looking at car headlights, streetlights, or any other white light.

✳ Make sure your eye is positioned correctly behind the eyepiece. You should see a clear and undistorted circular field of view, with the object you wish to observe inside that field. If your site is far from light pollution and if there is no moon in the sky, the sky will appear nearly black, so this field of view may be difficult to see.

If, on the other hand, there is scattered light in the sky, the field will appear gray and will reduce your ability to see very faint objects.

* Use averted vision when observing faint objects. Locate the object you wish to view in the center of your field and glance off to one side. In this way you'll be able to study the object's structure, or see detail that would be lost if you tried looking at it directly.

* Keep both eyes open. Most beginners automatically close one eye when using a telescope. They mistakenly think it helps them concentrate on the eye through which they are observing. In fact, all it does is tire the facial muscles, which will make you want to quit much sooner. Instead, train yourself to keep both eyes open but just look through the eye at the eyepiece. Naturally, this is much easier when it is very dark and there is no scattered light to distract the unused eye. But with some practice, you will become quite comfortable with one-eye vision.

With proper astronomical viewing techniques, even a small telescope can provide a lifetime of cosmic exploration.

Set up your telescope and begin observing at dusk so that you can become familiar with your surroundings before dark.

Keeping Records

Although you will become more and more familiar with the sky as you observe it, it changes in very subtle ways from night to night, season to season, and year to year. To make comparisons of what you see, you will want to take careful notes of your observations. Your logbook doesn't have to be fancy or elaborate; a simple notebook will do. Try to write down every significant thing you see with thorough detail.

Here are some things to include in your logbook records:

✓ date

✓ time

✓ number of the observing session

✓ sky conditions—seeing, transparency, phase of the moon

✓ instruments you used to make observation—star map, telescope, binocular

✓ who was with you (if anyone) at time of observation

✓ what you observed

✓ a complete description of any unusual sights

✓ drawing or photograph of phenomena

✓ the position and phase of the moon

In short, you want to write down anything that will help you remember what you saw, even years from the time you saw it.

A camera can be attached to a telescope to create the effect of a super telephoto lens, though a strong, rigid tripod is necessary.

Taking Photographs

Believe it or not, one of the best ways to keep records of the things you see in the night sky is to photograph them. You might think that objects in the heavens are much too far away and faint for you to get a good picture of them. But with simple equipment and a few useful techniques, it is possible to take beautiful, and very informative, photographs of the sky.

You can take pictures of the stars with any camera, but it is best to use a 35mm camera because you can control the exposure time for the photographs you take. Because the stars are so faint and give off very little light, it is most effective to take photos with a long time-exposure—at least 15 seconds.

Most 35mm cameras come with a normal 50mm lens. This is fine for sky photography, though a wide-angle lens may be even better. Don't bother investing in a longer focal-length lens (135mm or 200mm, for example); such lenses produce a higher magnification but with a very narrow field of view. You want to photograph as much of the sky as you can.

The third piece of equipment you need is a tripod, which will keep the camera steady during those long-exposure shots. You may even want a cable release to trigger the shutter, because pushing it yourself can cause the camera and tripod to vibrate, which will make your photographs blurry.

You can use any type of film you like—slide or print—but it should have a relatively high speed, say, ISO 400. Of course, the higher the film speed, the grainier the photographs will be, which is a problem if you want to enlarge them. Experiment to find the speed that works best for you from your observation site and is appropriate for what you are planning to do with the photographs.

When you look at your developed photographs or slides, don't be surprised to see all kinds of things that you didn't expect. First of all, objects that you didn't even see may show up in your photograph because the camera was able to gather enough light from them for them to show up. Second, your photographs may be ablaze with all kinds of colors that you didn't see. Film records light and color differently from the way the human eye does, so stars that appear white to our eyes may appear on film as a variety of colors, from red to yellow to blue. For this reason, even though the sky looks relatively black and white to your eye, use color film so that the film can reveal the color surprises the sky offers.

Star Maps

A star map is a scale model of the night sky during a certain season. It shows all the patterns of the stars and their locations relative to one another. Some star maps are quite simple, while others are very advanced and detailed. A simple star map is an essential tool for the beginning observer.

The sky changes constantly throughout the night, while the star maps, of course, do not. Instead, each map is a re-creation of the light sky in the early evening during a particular season. Each map is outlined by a circle that shows the horizon. At the map's center is a + mark that represents the overhead center point in the sky, known as the "zenith." Along the circle are marked the cardinal directions: north, south, east, and west. However, you will notice when looking down at the map that east and west are opposite of where it seems they should be. Don't worry; when you hold the map over your head they will be in the right places.

To read a star map, hold it over your head and align its cardinal directions with those on the real horizon. If you have selected the proper map, its stars should correspond closely with the real sky of early evening.

The black dots on the map represent the stars; the bigger the dot, the brighter the star. The recognizable groupings of stars are connected with dots. You will see some bright objects that do not appear on your star map. They are probably the planets, and they are not included on the star map because they constantly move through the sky. Finally, each star map features two illustrations, each of which contains dots of different sizes. The dots will help you see the key stars in each constellation.

*

Your eyes, a telescope (if you like), a star map, a notebook and pen, a red-colored flashlight, and a camera (again, optional), along with a lot of patience and perseverance, are all you need to have a really rewarding viewing session on almost any night. Just remember that the sky will reveal only as much as your sight and the night's conditions allow. Keep these conditions in mind and focus your session accordingly.

Using a Star Map

There are two ways to use a star map: going from sky to map, and going from map to sky. Both techniques are effective; it is just a matter of deciding which one suits your purpose.

To go from sky to map, locate the position of a particular bright star in the sky, then find it on the map, using the cardinal directions and zenith markers as guides. To go from map to sky, figure out from the chart where a particular star should be in the sky relative to the cardinal points and the other stars. Then look up and find it.

Another trick for finding your way around the sky is called "star hopping." With this technique, you use the stars you know to find the ones you don't know, moving from familiar star to familiar star until you find the new one. A common star hop in the Northern Hemisphere is to use the two stars at the end of the Big Dipper's bowl—from its bottom to its top—to point up to the bright star Polaris. Polaris, in turn, is the star at the tip of the Little Dipper's handle. On a dark night you can use Polaris to find the four stars in the Little Dipper's bowl that are of diminishing magnitude.

You can use this same method to move all around the sky. Just find a star you know, then figure out about how many degrees in a certain direction lies a star you don't know. Then use that star to find another.

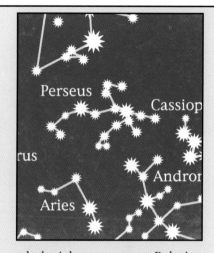

Above and left: The constellation Perseus offers the beginner a wealth of objects to view, including the variable star Algol and the famous double open star cluster.

Northern Hemisphere ✳ Spring

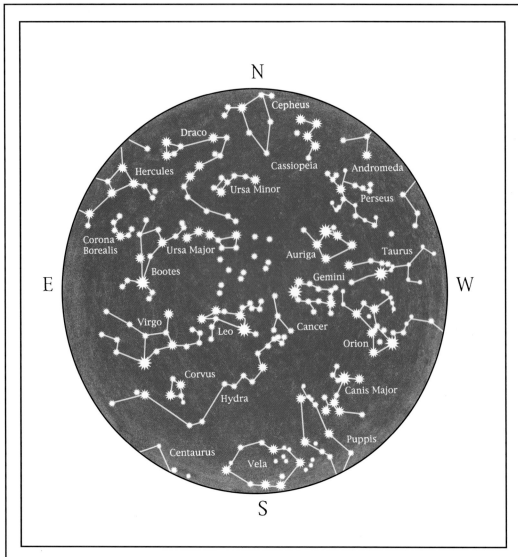

CANCER

URSA MINOR

Northern Hemisphere ✳ Summer

LIBRA

CORONA BOREALIS

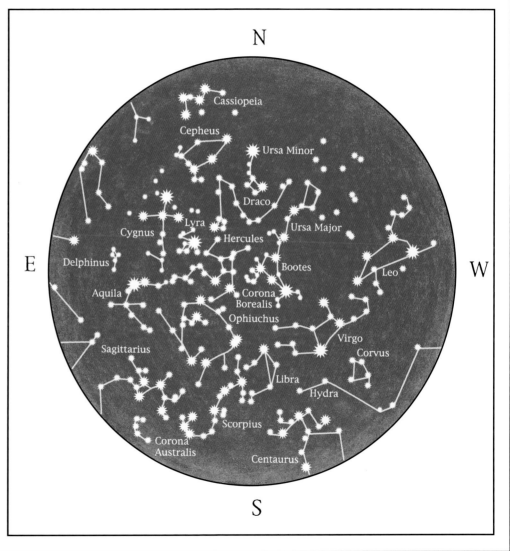

Northern Hemisphere ✷ Autumn

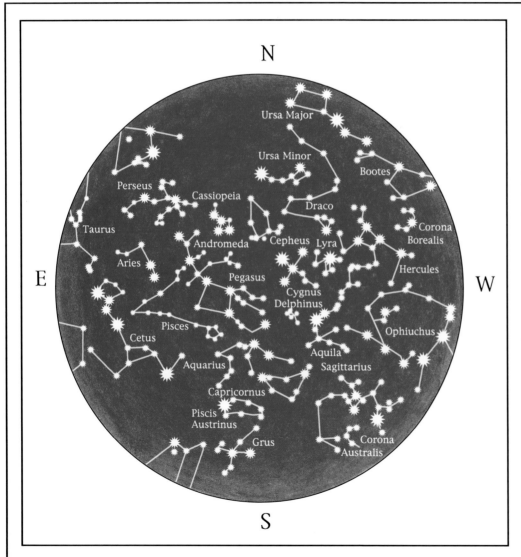

N

E

W

S

Ursa Major
Ursa Minor
Bootes
Perseus
Cassiopeia
Draco
Corona
Borealis
Taurus
Andromeda
Cepheus
Lyra
Aries
Hercules
Pegasus
Cygnus
Delphinus
Pisces
Ophiuchus
Cetus
Aquarius
Aquila
Sagittarius
Capricornus
Piscis
Austrinus
Grus
Corona
Australis

AQUARIUS

HERCULES

Northern Hemisphere ✷ Winter

GEMINI

CASSIOPEIA

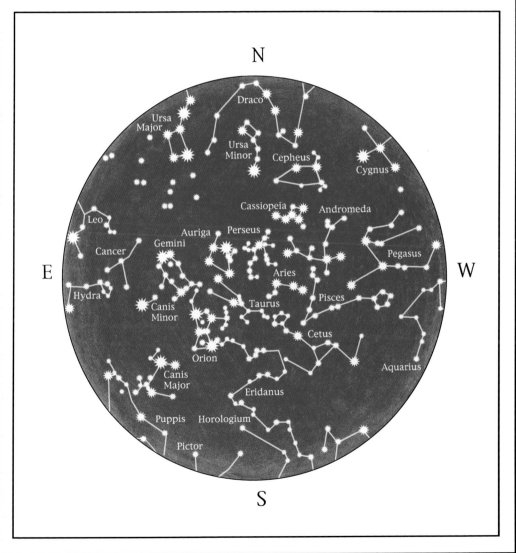

Southern Hemisphere ✴ Spring

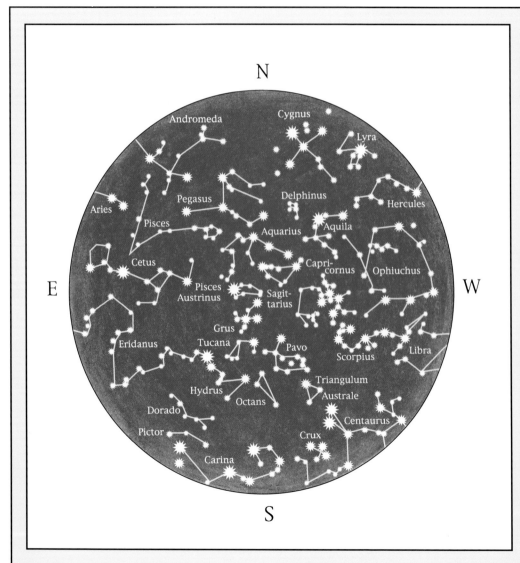

N

Andromeda
Cygnus
Lyra
Pegasus
Delphinus
Hercules
Aries
Pisces
Aquarius
Aquila
Cetus
Capri-
cornus
Ophiuchus
Pisces
Austrinus
Sagit-
tarius
Grus
Eridanus
Tucana
Pavo
Scorpius
Libra
Triangulum
Hydrus
Australe
Octans
Dorado
Centaurus
Pictor
Crux
Carina

E

W

S

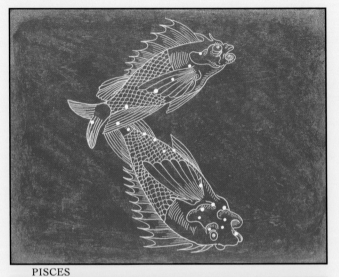

PISCES

DELPHINUS

Southern Hemisphere ✳ Summer

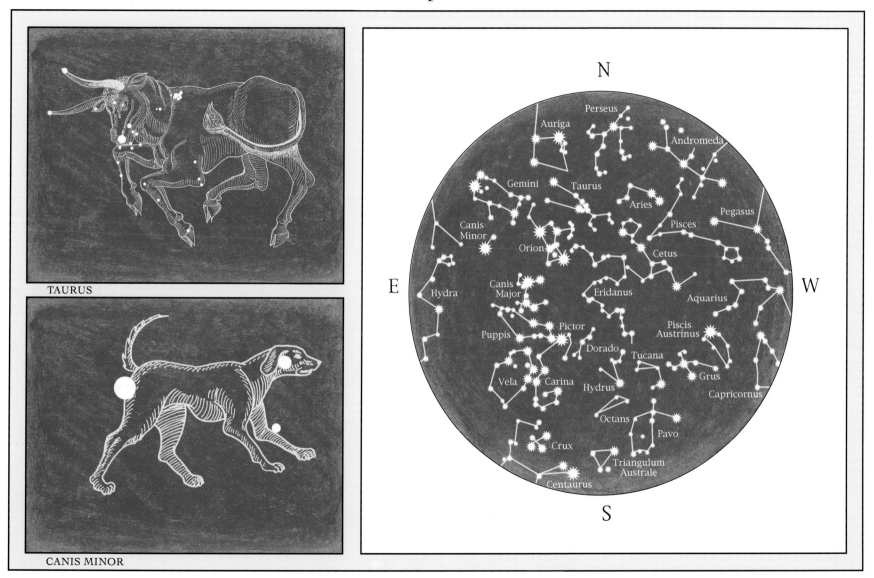

TAURUS

CANIS MINOR

N

E

W

S

Perseus

Auriga

Andromeda

Gemini

Taurus

Aries

Pegasus

Canis
Minor

Pisces

Orion

Cetus

Hydra

Canis
Major

Eridanus

Aquarius

Puppis

Pictor

Piscis
Austrinus

Dorado

Tucana

Vela

Carina

Hydrus

Grus

Capricornus

Octans

Pavo

Crux

Triangulum
Australe

Centaurus

Southern Hemisphere ✶ Autumn

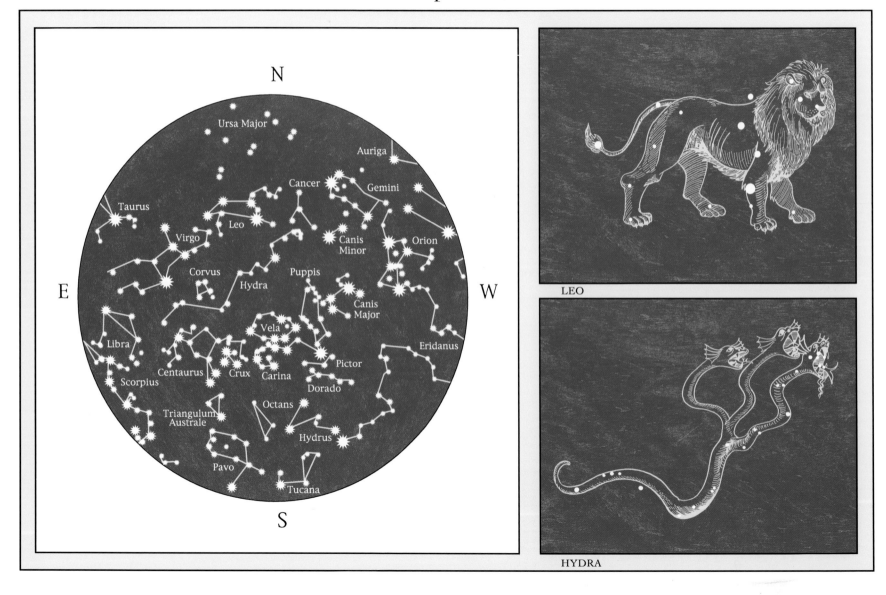

N

Ursa Major

Auriga

Cancer

Gemini

Taurus

Leo

Virgo

Canis
Minor

Orion

E

Corvus

Puppis

Hydra

W

Canis
Major

Vela

Libra

Eridanus

Centaurus

Crux

Pictor

Scorpius

Carina

Dorado

Triangulum
Australe

Octans

Hydrus

Pavo

Tucana

S

LEO

HYDRA

Southern Hemisphere ✷ Winter

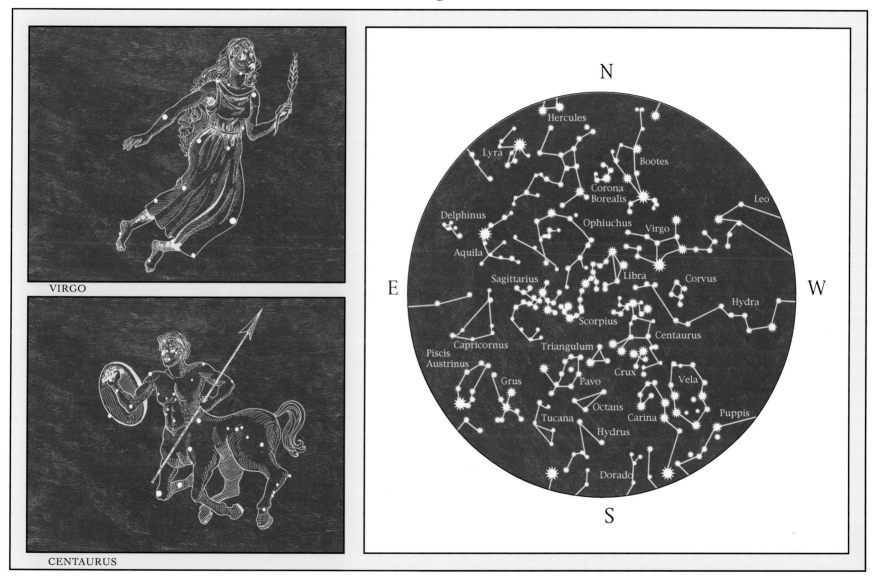

VIRGO

CENTAURUS

N

Hercules
Lyra
Bootes
Corona
Borealis
Leo
Delphinus
Ophiuchus
Virgo
Aquila
Sagittarius
Libra
Corvus
E
W
Scorpius
Hydra
Triangulum
Centaurus
Capricornus
Piscis
Austrinus
Crux
Vela
Grus
Pavo
Tucana
Octans
Carina
Puppis
Hydrus
Dorado
S

Chapter

Taking a Closer Look

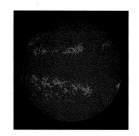

There comes a time for every beginning astronomer when observations with the naked eye just aren't good enough anymore. You want to see more, deeper, in greater detail. When that time comes, it is time to invest in a telescope.

Happily, the view offered by a simple, relatively inexpensive telescope is good enough to keep you fascinated for years and years. That said, selecting and purchasing that telescope can be frustrating and confusing. Telescopes come in a bewildering variety of types and sizes, as well as a range of prices.

It is easy to sort through all these choices and buy the right telescope for your situation if you approach the task by answering a few important questions. First, what do you wish to look at? Do you want to view the moon and the planets, or search for faint objects such as star clusters, nebulae, and galaxies? Another critical question is, how much do you want to spend? Use the answers to these questions to determine the best telescope for you, one that you will use and not just stuff in the hall closet.

How a Telescope Works

It is important to have some understanding of how a telescope works so that you can evaluate each model's features and compare advantages and disadvantages. Here is a simple description that will get you off to a good start.

Left: One of the accessories that can be added to a telescope is a solar filter, which fits over the front of the telescope aperture. ***Above:*** *Major observatories can take photographs of the sun in various wavelengths of light to produce many different images for study.*

A telescope aimed toward the sky gathers light, focuses it, and creates an image that can be studied by the eye or camera.

All telescopes work the same way: they gather faint light and concentrate it at a point where it is magnified into a finely detailed image. The most important property of a telescope is not its magnifying power, however, but its ability to gather light. The ability to gather light depends on the size of the telescope's main lens or mirror, known as its "objective." The larger the diameter of the objective, the more light the telescope can gather. For example, while a telescope with a 2.4-inch (60mm) -diameter objective will let you see ob- jects 100 times fainter than you could see with the unaided eye, one with a 4-inch (100mm) objective will help you see objects that are 251 times fainter. Not only does a larger telescope reveal fainter objects, but it presents them with greater clarity and in greater detail.

Once the light has been gathered, it is concentrated at the telescope's "focal point," then magnified by the eyepiece. The more an image is en- larged, the fainter it becomes. As you might imagine, there is a practical limit to a telescope's magnifying power. To find the maximum practical limit, multi- ply the telescope's diameter in inches by 50 (mm by 2). Calculating by means of this rule, the maximum usable magnifi- cation of a 4-inch (100mm) telescope is about 200X. Beware of a manufacturer or salesperson who boasts 600-power magnification on a 4-inch telescope. Magnifications over the maximum prac- tical limit aren't any good.

Also dependent upon a telescope's size is its ability to resolve fine detail in an image. A 2.4-inch (60mm) telescope can theoretically resolve craters on the moon 4 miles (6.4km) wide, while a 4-inch (100mm) telescope can theo- retically resolve craters only 2 miles (3.2km) wide.

Thus, it is fair to say that with telescopes, bigger is usually better. How- ever, bear in mind that, as with most delicate equipment, a finely made small telescope will outperform a poorly made large one.

Types of Telescopes

When you first start looking at tele- scopes, you will be faced with all kinds of strange-looking varieties. Only two kinds, the refractor and the reflector, are recommended for the beginner.

The refractor telescope resembles a spyglass. Light enters the front of its tube and is bent (refracted) by the objective lens and focused at the rear by the eyepiece. The advantages of the refractor for the beginning stargazer are that it is capable of producing high magnifications, and it often creates razor-sharp images of the moon and planets. It is also extremely rugged, re- sistant to misuse, and quite portable. One drawback is that its lens cannot fo- cus perfectly on all colors of light, so its images suffer from chromatic aberra- tion. In addition, refractor lenses are difficult and expensive to make, which means that smaller diameters—between 2 and 3 inches (50 and 76mm)—are more common. Still, a refractor tele- scope is perfect for the observer who wishes to concentrate on the moon, planets, and terrestrial activity.

The reflector telescope uses a highly polished mirror to gather starlight. There are several types of reflector telescopes, but the best for beginners are Newton- ian and rich-field reflectors.

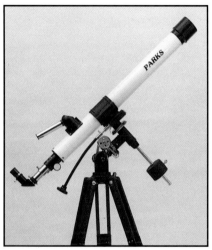

Two basic types of telescopes exist: the refractor **(top, left and right)** *uses lenses to collect and focus light, while the reflector* **(bottom, left and right)** *uses mirrors to collect and focus light.*

In the Newtonian-style reflector, light enters an open tube in front. At the back, the light encounters the primary mirror and is reflected back to a smaller, secondary mirror. The light is then reflected out the side of the tube to the eyepiece.

The relatively low magnifications and exceptionally wide-angle field of view of the rich-field reflector combine to produce brilliant and crisp images. Unlike the other types of telescopes, this one does not require a sturdy mounting; one model is even designed to be cradled in the arms.

Reflector telescopes are relatively inexpensive, which means that you can purchase a larger reflector for the same price as or less than a smaller refractor. Reflectors also give excellent color definition of all objects observed. Furthermore, their greater light-gathering power makes them suitable for viewing faint star clusters, nebulae, and galaxies.

The disadvantages of the reflectors are that they are not as rugged as the refractors, and their optics often need adjustment. Furthermore, because their tubes are open, they need to be very carefully stored.

Mountings

An important component of a telescope is its mounting, which holds the telescope steady during observation. A poor mounting will allow vibration from wind or even the observer's movements, which will blur the image. There are many kinds of mountings, but the two that are best for the beginner are the altitude-azimuth (or alt-az) mounting and the equatorial mounting.

The alt-az mounting is the most common, generally found on instruments 3 inches (76mm) in diameter or smaller. This mounting is similar to a camera tripod and can be moved in two directions: vertically (altitude) and horizontally (azimuth). The disadvantage of the alt-az mounting is that it requires the observer to make two separate adjustments to follow an object during the night. This is particularly annoying to do while watching an object for a very long period; you must keep making these two adjustments as it moves across the sky.

The equatorial mounting, on the other hand, is designed to simulate Earth's rotation exactly. With only one

sweeping movement, the observer can track an object through the night. In addition, the equatorial mounting is often marked with celestial coordinates to help aim the telescope. Of course, the equatorial mounting is designed for more serious stargazing and is therefore much more expensive than the alt-az.

Several basic types of telescope mountings exist. **Top:** *An equatorial mounting on a tripod allows smooth motion to follow an object as it moves it across the sky.* **Bottom, right:** *Here, an equatorial mounting sits on a pedestal, which can be much more solid and vibration-free than a tripod.* **Bottom, left:** *An alt-az fork mounting can hold large telescopes in a relatively compact package.*

Many sizes, types, and focal lengths of eyepieces are available; these have imprints on them telling the type and focal length of each.

Stargazing Accessories

Telescopes can be enhanced with any number of accessories. Of course, having a telescope at all will be challenge enough for the beginner. Here's the lowdown on some of the features that may come with your telescope so that you will know how to use them when you are ready.

Most telescopes are equipped with the two essential accessories: a finderscope and a set of eyepieces. A finderscope is a small 5X or 6X telescope mounted parallel to the main tube near the eyepiece holder. It has an exceptionally wide field of view and crosshairs that let you locate and center objects for study in the main instrument.

As well as allowing you to see through the telescope, the particular eyepiece you use determines the magnifying power. Most telescopes come with three eyepieces: one of low-power magnification (20X to 50X), one of medium power (50X to 100X), and one of high power (100X or more). To determine the magnification power of each eyepiece, divide the number printed on its side (the focal length) into the focal length of the telescope (printed on the side of the telescope or in the instruction manual). For example, a 900mm focal-length telescope with a 20mm focal-length eyepiece would produce a magnification of 45X.

You will use the low-power eyepiece much more than you will the high-power eyepiece. The low-power eyepiece has a wider field of view and is more useful for locating and observing faint objects. High-power eyepieces have a narrow field of view and are useful only when you are viewing a bright object on a steady night.

Many telescopes also come with a sun filter, which screws onto the bottom of the eyepiece. *These filters are extremely dangerous and should be discarded at once.* Manufacturers claim that using a sun filter makes it possible to observe the sun. You should know that these filters can melt, burn, or crack, then throw a scorching beam of sunlight directly to your eye, which can cause instant blindness. Sun filters that fit over the telescope tube itself are available and safe.

Moon filters (not to be confused with sun filters), which also often come with telescopes, are perfectly safe for lunar observation. They are not necessary, but you might find that they cut down on the glare and improve the contrast of a bright moon.

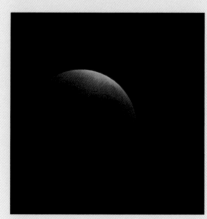

A lunar eclipse nearing totality.

Checklist for Purchasing a Telescope

When you have narrowed down your selections, run each model through the following checklist:

✓ Make sure the image the telescope displays is bright and clear.
✓ Make sure there is minimal distortion and minimal chromatic aberration.
✓ Make sure the tripod and mounting are sturdy.
✓ Make sure the controls are easy to reach.
✓ Make sure the control knobs move easily.
✓ Make sure the telescope is lightweight and portable.
✓ Make sure the finderscope is attached to the telescope.
✓ Make sure that the telescope comes with accessory eyepieces and that each one displays a sharp image.

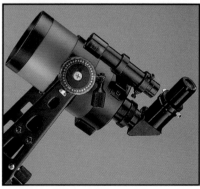

Top: *When purchasing a telescope, make sure its tripod is solid; any vibration will be translated to the image.*
Bottom: *A telescope should have an attached finderscope, and all controls should be within easy reach.*

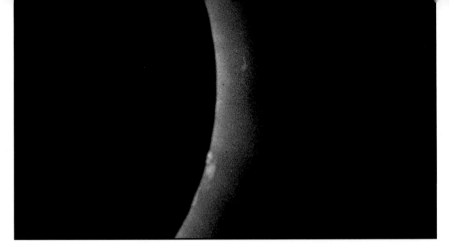

*Above: During a total solar eclipse, a telescope can show a tremendous amount of detail that would be invisible at any other time. **Opposite:** To a telescope, the Milky Way is resolved into myriad stars, star clusters, and interstellar clouds.*

Secondhand May Be Just Fine

If you find the prices of the telescopes you like to be prohibitive, think about buying a used one. Astronomers are upgrading all the time, which means the model they are trading in could be just perfect for you. It may take a little patience to find exactly the one you want, but it will be worth it if you save a lot of money. Visit shops that sell used telescopes, and let the salespeople know what you are looking for. Often, they will be happy to give you a call as soon as they get one in so that you can have the best shot at purchasing it. Also keep an eye on the ads in your local paper or the newsletter of a local amateur astronomy group.

When you find a telescope that you like, examine it carefully and run it through the "Checklist for Purchasing a Telescope" on page 71. If it meets these standards, you probably have a really good instrument at a great price.

Using Your Telescope

No matter how fine a telescope you buy, how you use it will affect its performance. One of the most important things you can do is store it carefully when it is not in use. If it is exposed to dirt or often jostled, it can be damaged. Store it in its case in a place where no one will be moving it.

The next consideration is setting it up properly. It is best to do this well before dark so that you can see exactly what you are doing and what the terrain is like. Assemble your telescope on a solid piece of ground. (Try to avoid asphalt; it absorbs heat during the day and radiates it at night, which may cause distortions in front of your telescope.) Make sure the telescope is level and the mounting is solidly assembled.

Next, align the finderscope with the telescope. To do this, aim your telescope at a very distant object, such as a mountaintop or a radio antenna. Put on a low-power eyepiece and find the object in the telescope. Then switch to the higher-power eyepiece and align it so that a recognizable feature is directly in the center of its field of view. Lock down the telescope so it can't move. Next, loosen the finderscope and point it so that the crosshairs are aimed at the same object, then lock it in place. Now you are ready to use the finderscope to help you discover the mysteries of the sky.

As darkness falls and the stars begin to appear, your eyes will become dark-adapted. Use this time to focus your telescope. To do this, aim your telescope on a star of 2nd or 3rd magnitude. Turn the telescope focus knob one way, and watch as the star turns larger and fuzzier. Turn it the other way; if the star looks like a fuzzy ring, the telescope is not focused properly. Keep turning the knob until the star appears as a tiny and sharp point of light.

Next, use the focused telescope to check the seeing and transparency of the sky. Aim it toward a star high overhead and notice how much it twinkles. Then aim toward a star of similar magnitude low in the sky. You should see a significant difference in the stars' scintillation. Use your observations of the seeing and transparency to help you determine your best specimens for the evening's session.

✳

With a little patience, determination, and practice, the sky is the limit in astronomy. You can always look deeper and farther. The heavens are constantly changing, revealing new secrets and mysteries. Now that you know the basics, the heavens are yours to explore and enjoy.

Sources

Periodicals and Magazines

Abrams Planetarium Sky Calendar.
Published quarterly, $7.50 per year.

Sky Calendar
Abrams Planetarium
Michigan State University
East Lansing, MI 48824

Set of monthly star charts; includes a daily guide for watching astronomical events.

Astronomy magazine. 12 issues per year, $26.95 in the U.S.; $38.00 outside the U.S.

Kalmbach Publishing
21027 Crossroads Circle
P.O. Box 1612
Waukesha, WI 53187-1612

An advanced journal on current events in the world of astronomy.

Odyssey magazine. 9 issues per year, $22.95 in the U.S.; $30.95 outside the U.S.

Cobblestone Publishing
7 School Street
Peterborough, NH 03458

For young readers 8 to 14 years old and beginning astronomers; includes sky games and activities.

Sky and Telescope magazine. 12 issues per year, $33.00 in U.S.; $50.00 in England; $43.00 in Australia

40-50-51 Bay State Road
Cambridge, MA 02238

A hands-on journal for the actual sky observer; includes articles about new equipment and ways of observing the night sky.

Astronomy Organizations and Societies

United States

Astronomical Society of the Pacific
390 Ashton Avenue
San Francisco, CA 94112

The Planetary Society
65 North Catalina Avenue
Pasadena, CA 91106

Australia

Astronomy Society of NSW
Box 208 Eastwood, NSW 2122

Astronomy Society of Victoria
Box 1059J GPO
Melbourne 3001

Canada

Canadian Amateur Astronomers
417 Foch Avenue
Windsor, Ontario N8X 2W2

Royal Astronomical Society of Canada
124 Merton Street
Toronto, Ontario M4S 2Z2

England

British Astronomical Association
Burlington House
Piccadilly, London W1V 9AG

British Interplanetary Society
12 Bessbourough GDS
London SW1V 2JJ

Computer Software

Dance of the Planets (for IBM and compatibles)

ARC Software
P.O. Box 1955
Loveland, CO 80539

The Sky (for IBM and compatibles)

Software Bisque
912 Twelfth Street
Golden, CO 80401

Voyager (for Macintosh)

Carina Software
830 Williams Street
San Leandro, CA 94577

Bibliography

Clairborne, Robert. *The Summer Stargazer*. New York: Coward, McCann & Geoghegan, Inc., 1975.

Covington, Michael. *Astrophotography for the Amateur*. New York: Cambridge University Press, 1991.

Dickinson, Terry. *Exploring the Night Sky*. Camden East, Ont.: Camden House Publishing, 1987.

Eastman Kodak. *Astrophotography Basics*. Rochester, N.Y.: Eastman Kodak, 1988.

Hamburg, Michael. *Astronomy Made Simple*. New York: Stonesong Press, 1993.

Harrington, Sherwood. *Selecting a First Telescope*. San Francisco: Astronomical Society of the Pacific, 1988.

Mallas, John, and Evered Kreimer. *The Messier Album*. Cambridge, Mass.: Sky Publishing Corporation, 1978.

Mammana, Dennis. *The Night Sky*. Philadelphia: Running Press, 1989.

Martin, Martha Evans, and Donald Howard Menzel. *The Friendly Stars*. New York: Dover Publications, Inc., 1966.

Mayall, R. Newton, and Margaret Mayall. *Skyshooting: Photography for the Amateur Astronomer*. New York: Dover Publications, Inc., 1968.

Nourse, Alan E. *The Backyard Astronomer*. New York: Franklin Watts, Inc., 1973.

Peltier, Leslie. *Starlight Nights*. Cambridge, Mass.: Sky Publishing Corporation, 1980.

Zim, Herbert S., and Robert H. Baker. *Stars*. New York: Golden Press, 1985.

Glossary

Altitude: The measure, usually in degrees, of an object's height above the horizon.

Altitude-azimuth (alt-az) mounting: A telescope mounting in which one axis is parallel to the ground and the other is perpendicular to it.

Annular eclipse: A solar eclipse in which a ring of the sun appears to surround the smaller, darker moon.

Apogee: The point in the orbit of an object at which it is farthest from Earth.

Asterism: A group of stars that forms the outline of something familiar, such as Orion's belt. An asterism can be part of a constellation. *See* **Constellation.**

Asteroid: A chunk of iron or rock that orbits the sun.

Averted vision: Viewing an object with the side of the retina or the rods. A technique used to observe very faint objects.

Azimuth: The measure, usually in degrees, of an object's position along the horizon; usually measured eastward from the north.

Bolide: A brilliant meteor that smokes, whistles, or explodes during its fall through the atmosphere.

Chromatic aberration: A flaw in the way that a telescope sees color.

Comet: A chunk of ice that orbits the sun in an elliptical path; often has a long, glowing tail of cosmic debris.

Constellation: An arbitrary area of the sky that resembles a person, thing, or animal, recognized from ancient times.

Corona: The outer atmosphere of the sun that can be seen only during a total solar eclipse.

Crater: A bowl-shaped scar on a planet or satellite caused by an asteroid or comet smashing into it.

Dark adaptation: A condition in which the eyes have adjusted to see in darkness by widening the pupils so they can admit as much light as possible.

Degree: An angular measure equal to $1/360$ of a circle. One degree in astronom-ical terms is approximately equal to the width of the little finger, viewed held up to the sky at arm's length.

Eclipsing binary: A double-star system wherein one star, periodically, partially or totally eclipses the light from the other star.

Elliptical orbit: A path that looks like a flattened circle.

Equatorial mounting: A telescope mounting in which one axis is parallel to Earth's axis and the other is perpen-dicular to it.

Falling star: *See* **Meteor**.

Field of view: The area of the sky visi-ble through a telescope or camera.

Focal length: The distance on a tele-scope between the center of a lens or mirror and the focus.

Galaxy: A collection of hundreds of bil-lions of stars, star clusters, and clouds of dust and gas held together by gravita-tional forces. The Milky Way is our galaxy.

Globular star cluster: A tightly packed ball of thousands or millions of stars.

Horizon: The imaginary line that joins the sky and the ground. The true horizon can be seen only on the open ocean.

Large Magellanic Cloud (LMC): One of two nearby galaxies to the Milky Way that appear as amorphous patches of light among the stars of the Southern Hemisphere.

Light pollution: Light from streetlights, headlights, and other sources of artifical light that shines into the sky and makes it difficult to see faint stars.

Light-year: The distance light travels in a year, equal to 6 trillion miles (9.6 trillion km).

Lunar eclipse: A phenomenon that oc-curs when the moon passes into the shadow of Earth and disappears tem-porarily from view.

Magnitude: The brightness of a star as we see it. A 1st-magnitude star is as bright as a candle flame burning $1/4$ mile (0.4km) away. The larger the numerical value of the magnitude, the fainter the object.

Meteor: A speck of dust that burns up as it falls into our atmosphere; also called a falling star or a shooting star.

Meteorite: A chunk of iron or rock that has fallen from space to Earth.

Meteoroid: A piece of dust, rock, or iron tumbling through space.

Meteor shower: Meteors that appear to rain from a certain point in the sky over the course of several nights; caused by the collision of Earth's atmosphere with a stream of interplanetary particles.

Milky Way: The hazy band of light we see in the night sky. The Milky Way forms the plane of the galaxy in which we live; all stars seen at night belong to it.

Nebula: A cloud of gas and dust in space. Nebulae are sometimes illuminated by the stars around them or embedded in them.

Objective: The primary mirror in a reflector telescope, or the front or principal lens in a refractor telescope.

Opposition: When a celestial body lies on the opposite side of the sky from the sun. The full moon, for example, occurs at opposition.

Orbit: The path an object takes when revolving around another object.

Perigee: The point in the orbit of an object at which it is closest to Earth.

Phase: The shape an object seems to have as the light falling on it changes.

Planet: A body more than 600 miles (960km) in diameter that orbits around the sun and shines by reflecting sunlight.

Reflector telescope: An instrument that uses a mirror to gather light from the sky and focuses that light into an image an observer can magnify and study.

Refractor telescope: An instrument that uses a lens to gather light from the sky and focuses that light into an image an observer can magnify and study.

Satellite: A natural or man-made object revolving around another object, such as a planet or a moon; called a "moon" if it is not man-made.

Scintillation: The rapid and irregular movement of a star's image caused by the turbulent atmosphere around us; commonly known as "twinkling."

Seeing: A measure of the atmosphere's steadiness, taken by comparing the scintillation of different objects in the sky. *See* **Scintillation**.

Shooting star: *See* **Meteor**.

Small Magellanic Cloud (SMC): One of two nearby galaxies to the Milky Way that appear as amorphous patches of light among the stars of the Southern Hemisphere.

Solar eclipse: A phenomenon that occurs when the moon passes between Earth and the sun, temporarily blocking the sunlight and casting the moon's shadow on Earth.

Solar system: The sun and all the objects held in its gravitational field.

Spiral galaxy: A galaxy in the shape of a pinwheel.

Star cluster: A family of stars held together by gravity.

Star hopping: An astronomical trick used to find a star or group of stars by using other stars as pointers.

Sunspots: Dark spots on the face of the sun that appear to move and change as the sun rotates.

Twinkling: *See* **Scintillation**.

Variable star: A star whose luminosity appears to change with time.

Zenith: The point in the sky directly overhead.

Zodiac: The band of stars and constellations through which our sun, moon, and planets appear to travel. The zodiac has twelve constellations.

Zodiacal light: A triangular haze of light that appears in our sky, caused by the reflected light from tiny particles along the plane of our solar system.

78

Photo Credits

©**Bay Photo:** p. 26 right

Courtesy of Celestron International:
pp. 21 right, 28, 29 top, 30, 31 top left

©**Mark Coco:** pp. 9, 33 top right

Dembinsky Photo Associates:
©**John Gerlach:** p. 22 right; ©**Russ Gutshall:** p. 24; ©**Stan Osolinsky:** p. 48

©**George East:** p. 25 both

©**H.M. Heyn:** p. 51 left

©**Richard Hill:** pp. 50 left, 55 right

©**Alan McClure:** pp. 16, 17

©**Dennis Milon:** p. 15 left

©**Alan E. Morton:** pp. 15 right, 49 right

©**NASA:** pp. 20, 37 left, 39 both, 40, 41 both

Courtesy National Optical Astronomy Observatories: pp. 5 top, 51 right, 67

All star maps and diagrams on pp. 57–65 by **Emilya Naymark**

Courtesy of Orion Telescopes & Binoculars ©1995: pp. 55 left, 70 top and right

©**John R. Peckham:** p. 50 right

©**Photo Network, Tustin:** pp. 2, 45 right; ©**Astrostock/Sanford:** pp. 6, 8, 12 both, 57; ©**Dr. Jean Dragosco/ Sanford:** p. 31 bottom left; ©**JPL/ NASA/Astrostock/Sanford:** pp. 35; ©**John Sanford:** pp. 13, 14, 26 left, 32, 33 bottom right, 37 right, 42, 52,53, 66, 69 top right, 70 bottom left and right

©**Frank Rossotto:** pp. 18, 19, 54

©**Sherman Schultz:** p. 72

©**Tom Stack and Associates:**
©**ESA/TSADO:** p. 29 bottom; ©**Bill and Sally Fletcher:** pp. 3, 7, 10, 23, 45 middle; ©**John Gerlach:** p. 22 left; ©**JPL/TSADO:** pp. 18 left, 34, 36 both; ©**NASA/TSADO:** p. 27; ©**NASA Hubble/Airworks:** p. 45 right; ©**NOAO:** p. 75; ©**NOAA/TSADO:** pp. 31 right, 44 both, 47; ©**Mike O'Brine:** pp. 5 bottom, 43 right, 46 left, 71 left, 73; ©**Greg Vaughn:** p. 33 left

Courtesy of Swift Instruments, Inc., Boston, MA: pp. 5 middle, 56, 68, 69 top left and bottom left and right, 71 top and bottom right

Index